IMPLEMENTING
STRATEGIC CHANGE

IMPLEMENTING STRATEGIC CHANGE

Tools for Transforming an Organization

Steven H. Hoisington

S. A. Vaneswaran

McGraw-Hill

New York Chicago San Francisco Lisbon London Madrid Mexico
City Milan New Delhi San Juan Seoul Singapore Sydney Toronto

CONTENTS

PREFACE

The Minnesota Council for Quality and the College of Continuing Education at the University of Minnesota surveyed Council members to better understand what quality/improvement topics were of interest to the marketplace. The University of Minnesota used the results of the survey to develop appropriate open enrollment courses; the Council uses it to identify other potential programs or services that might add value to its members.

The top ten topics (based on a 5-point scale, where 5 indicated "very interested" and 1 indicated "very disinterested") are as follows:

1. Tools/Approaches for Managing and Improving Organization's Performance (4.15)

2. Strategic Planning (4.00)

3. Balanced Scorecard and Performance Management (3.91)

4. Change Management (3.84)

5. Leadership Development (3.74)

6. Customer Relationship Management (3.65)

7. Six Sigma (3.57)

8. Knowledge Management (3.51)

9. Malcolm Baldrige National Quality Award (3.37)

10. Quality/TQM (3.28)

This book was not written to address the results of this survey, but it is interesting to note that these results surfaced during similar surveys conducted in the past decade.

This book provides a discussion on major topics impacting an organization that is grappling with the concept of change management and the need to significantly improve performance. Many organizations, in the context of rapidly changing market dynamics and fierce competition, need not only to be responsive to these changes but also continue to re-strategize on an ongoing basis if they are to maintain a leading edge. In trying to translate that objective into reality, most organizations remain clueless and wrestle with "solutions of the day" or "flavors of the month" or "program of the year" that often end up being less than effective. You can hear their mantra of wanting to be like a GE or an IBM without investing the required time, energy, and resources on improvement.

In the opinion and experience of the authors, there is no book that attempts to recommend a "solution" that will guide organizations, through the language of Customer Driven Quality, to remain competitively superior at all times. This book attempts to assess the pros and cons of various models such as re-engineering, Six Sigma and the Malcolm Baldrige National Quality Award criteria that are used to assess and guide an organization's overall performance. The authors will also define a customer-focused, customer-centered culture, and explain different methods to establish and reinforce this behavior throughout all levels of the organization.

The target audience for this book include corporate managers and senior executives, business development professionals in the manufacturing and service sector (hardware and software), and quality professionals. Because of the various examples illustrated, it can be used as a "how to" manual in organizations. Its applicability also extends to the classroom, where it can be used as a business or quality textbook.

The chapters in this book are based on the following salient points:

1. Stress on the need to create and enhance customer and shareholder value. Thus, any organizational transformation program should focus on identifying areas for improvement and implementing solutions to maximize value. Improvement programs that are inward focused seldom stand the test of time.

2. Present an integrated approach that explains how to make best use of the most vogue and available approaches such as Economic Value-Added (EVA), Baldrige, Balanced Scorecard, and Six Sigma. This book provides an insight into the pragmatic use of these techniques. When integrated into a composite transformation program, these approaches deliver value as opposed to their use in a stand alone mode—a practice deployed by most companies.

3. A departure from conventional quality management philosophy with a stress on the fact that process/business improvements across the organization need to be aligned to rapidly changing environments. Thus, it is important to focus on implementing a flexible and agile strategy development framework coupled with an improvement program that can yield short as well as long-term business benefits for all stakeholders.

4. A pragmatic and application-oriented discussion on the Baldrige process, with a focus on using the model for structured organizational assessments/diagnostics. While the model has much strength, this book focuses on how to use it to align and integrate improvements.

5. A brief discussion on other Baldrige-based assessment models such as European Foundation for Quality Management (EFQM) and Software Engineering Institute (SEI).

6. Clarify that while the Baldrige is an assessment tool, the Balanced Scorecard is an implementation tool. The Balanced Scorecard creates a strategy management framework which is important to manage key improvement initiatives. This will be illustrated through examples.

7. Elaborate upon the value of Six Sigma as a problem-solving tool and illustrate how it can be used to bring about process improvements on prioritized processes arising out of the earlier steps. While there is much mystery and myth around the Six Sigma approach, the authors attempt to demystify the same through insights into simple, yet effective, implementation practices.

8. A brief discussion on corporate governance that attempts to bring in a paradigm shift by judging the organization performance on both financial and non-financial dimensions through institutionalization of the Balanced Scorecard approach.

The authors have tried to present as many real-life examples as possible and offer many references to additional sources of information on related topics. All the data and examples presented in this book are real or based on real situations and organizations. In some cases, it was necessary to disguise the data for proprietary reasons. Our belief is that actual data is richer and more realistic than made up data. Where possible, the actual names of organizations are included, but in some situations, that was simply not possible.

We trust the readers will share our belief that business transformation is a requirement for any organization in today's fast-paced environment, and that a number of models and methods exist to facilitate organizational change. The authors believe, based on past experiences of working directly with a number of organizations that have gone through major transformations, that the tools and techniques used must be carefully considered, that the organization should never lose sight of its values and beliefs, that customers must always come and remain first, and that change is inevitable.

ACKNOWLEDGMENTS

Writing a book is an arduous task that requires the support of many. The authors thank colleagues, coworkers, and friends who provided advice and encouragement during the three years it took to finish the book. Special contributions were provided by Dr. Tze-His (Sam) Huang of IBM for statistical correlation of non-financial and financial measurements shown in Appendix A, Sanjay Purohit of Infosys for information on Assessing Organizational Capability in Chapter 3 and Balanced Scorecard in Chapter 6, and Hilla Singh of 3 Communications for information on SEI/CMM Model in Chapter 4. The authors also wish to thank Joseph Fumo of Joseph Fumo, Inc., Milwaukee, Wisconsin, for his assistance in editing and proofreading the manuscript.

Steve Hoisington acknowledges his fellow Malcolm Baldrige National Quality Award and Wisconsin State Forward Award examiners, his friends and colleagues at IBM and Johnson Controls, Inc., and his peers with the New Zealand Quality Award, Minnesota Quality Award, Infosys, and Tata Quality Management Services for providing him with the opportunities, knowledge, and experiences that made this book possible. Encouragement and support of family and close friends helped maintain the focus necessary to complete the book.

S.A. Vaneswaran would like to thank and acknowledge his friends and well wishers at the Tata Group in India for the opportunities that were made available to him. It would not be out of place to mention that the genesis on the need for a book of this nature came as a result of discussions with some of the Senior Management in the Tata Group a few years back. Thanks are also due to many of the

Executives, peers and friends at Lucent Technologies, Infosys, and Tata Quality Management Services who were a source of constant encouragement right from the very beginning.

The authors dedicate this book to their families, but especially to their sons Lenny, Ajay, and Anand.

ACRONYMS

#	Number
AIAG	Automotive Industry Action Group
AOP	Annual Operating Plans
APQP	Advanced Quality Planning and Control Plan
BB	Black Belts
BSC	Balanced Scorecard
BSI	British Standards Institute
Capex	Capital Expenses
CLI	Customer Loyalty Index
CMM	Capability Maturity Model
CRM	Customer Relationship Management
CSA	Canadian Standards Association
DCR	Data Confirmation Reports
DMAIC	Define, Measure, Analyze, Improve , Control
DNV	Det Norske Veritas
DPPM	Defects in Parts per Million
EFQM	European Foundation for Quality Management
EVA	Economic Value-Added
FMEA	Failure Mode and Effects Analysis
GPP	Global Performance Platform
HOQ	House of Quality
ISO	International Organization for Standardization
ISS	Institutional Shareholder Services
KPI	Key Performance Indicator
KRA	Key Result Area
PPAP	Production Part Approval Process
KPA	Key Performance Area
MRS	Metrics Repository Service
MSA	Measurement System Analysis
NIST	National Institute of Standards and Technology

NOPAT	Net Operating Profit after Tax
NPI	New Product Introduction
OQL	Order Quality Level
PAT	Profit after Tax
QFD	Quality Function Deployment
QSA	Quality System Audit
QSR	Quality System Review
R&D	Research and Development
RA's	Repair Actions—Corrections made to hardware installed in customer locations
RADAR	Results, Approach, Deployment, Assessment, and Review
ROCE	Return on Capital Employed
ROI	Return on Investment
S&P	Standard and Poor's
SBU	Strategic Business Unit
SEC	Securities and Exchange Commission
SEI	Software Engineering Institute
SIC	Standard Industrial Code
SP	Systems Products
SS	Sales and Service
SWOT	Strengths, Weaknesses, Opportunities, Threats
TFVUA's	Total Field Valid Unique APARS—Customer-discovered software defects
TQM	Total Quality Management
UL	Underwriters Laboratories
UTD	University of Texas, Dallas
WACC	Weighted Average Cost of Capital
WIIFM	What's In It For Me

LIST OF ILLUSTRATIONS

IMPLEMENTING
STRATEGIC CHANGE

□

DEVELOPING A CUSTOMER-FOCUSED CULTURE

INTERNAL AND EXTERNAL FACTORS AFFECTING ORGANIZATIONS

For most organizations, becoming more customer-focused is not a matter of choice. There are a number of factors that impact an organization and cause it to assess its approach toward regular interactions with customers. Figure 1.1 illustrates a number of internal and external factors that an organization must deal with on a regular basis.[1] Global competition is one of the most compelling reasons for an organization to become (more) customer focused. If business opportunities exist, and customers are readily available, competitors will sprout overnight. Even if an organization is in a marketplace or industry where there is no competition, for example, governmental agencies or educational institutions, there will be competition for resources and skills. In addition, whether or not competition exists, customers expect an organization to get better over time. Customers (citizens) do not expect taxes to be raised, tuitions to be increased, or prices to be hiked. They expect organizations

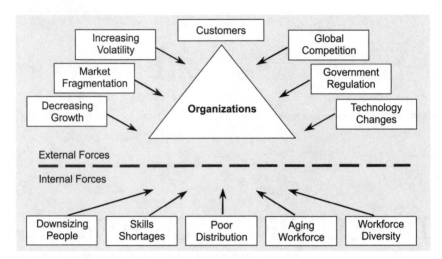

Fig. 1.1   Internal and External Factors Affecting Organizations

to understand what is important to them and deliver on those factors. Customers feel entitled to certain levels of outcome and service.

Industry and customers also drive the need for an organization to become more customer focused. Some industries are turning to strategies that enhance a customer-focused culture and, as a differentiator, offer more or better customer service. This, in turn, increases the expectations of all customers. Again, an environment of "entitlement" results from one organization delivering a higher level of performance. There is an old adage about the "price of admission" or the expected "cost of doing business." If one organization raises the bar of expected performance, what once seemed extraordinary becomes the standard for doing business.

There are changes that occur in an organization on a regular basis, in which the organization has little or no control. Government or industry regulations, certifications, and laws can change how an organization operates or how a product or service is developed, manufactured, or delivered. In many industries, technology changes occur on a frequent basis. They result in change within an organization. In time, these changes become the norm and are expected by customers. If an organization is customer-focused, it will embrace these changes quickly in order to meet the expectations of its customers. If they are truly customer-focused, they will anticipate these changes or play the role of a catalyst in implementing these changes as industry standards.

It is possible that your organization is already the best in its business and you want to keep it that way. The way to stay ahead of the pack is to enhance your organization's focus on customers. It is difficult to go out of business if you have a constant stream of income from existing customers. Studies have shown that customer retention increases as their satisfaction levels increase. In other words, the more delighted your customers, the less likely they are to defect. This concept is illustrated in Figure 1.2.[2]

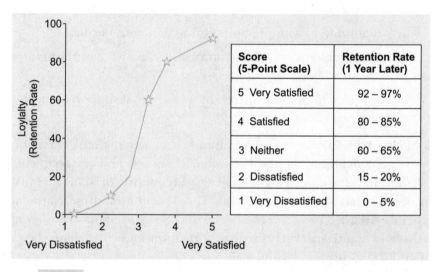

Score (5-Point Scale)	Retention Rate (1 Year Later)
5 Very Satisfied	92 – 97%
4 Satisfied	80 – 85%
3 Neither	60 – 65%
2 Dissatisfied	15 – 20%
1 Very Dissatisfied	0 – 5%

Fig. 1.2   Relationship between Customer Retention and Satisfaction

WHAT IS A CUSTOMER?

There has been an endless debate on the identity of a customer. As the final arbiter, customers are the reason the organization exists. They are the reason we all come to work everyday. Some organizations consider the person working next to you a customer. For purposes of defining and creating a customer-focused culture, a customer is defined as external to the organization and one who provides revenue to keep the organization operational. This definition could include taxpayers, students or parents who pay tuition, or the person or organization that purchases your products and/or services.

WHAT CONSTITUTES CUSTOMER-FOCUSED BEHAVIOR

The following behaviors describe a customer-focused environment:

- An understanding of customer needs/expectations
- Meeting or exceeding the expectations of customers
- Aligning value-creating processes around the customer
- A business philosophy of delivering ever-increasing value to customers
- An attitude of winning and putting the customer first
- A comprehensive effort, strategic initiative, and ongoing process
- A cultural imperative driven by a vision that supports a strong focus on customers

There are a number of organizations that come to mind when one mentions the phrase "customer-focused". Many of these are recipients of the Malcolm Baldrige National Quality Award[3] or similar award programs that are Baldrige based. The Malcolm Baldrige National Quality Award criteria devotes one of its seven categories to being customer (and market) focused. Organizations that have been identified as leaders by the Baldrige criteria demonstrate a strong correlation between its customer focus and business results. The higher the focus on customers, the greater the sustainability of an organization. In other words, there is a direct correlation between an organization's focus on its customers, its longevity, and its success in business. Examples include IBM and Hewlett-Packard; both formed on the foundation of providing superior customer service. According to findings of the Baldrige National Quality Program office, being "customer-focused" is a core value embedded in the beliefs and behaviors of high-performance organizations.

Definitions of Customer-Focused Behavior

The Malcolm Baldrige National Quality Award has identified the key factors associated with being customer-focused. They are:

- Knowledge about current customers

- Knowledge about potential customers and customers of competitors

- Proactive systems that support customers

- Multiple methods of listening to customers and gathering requirements including:

  ❑ Surveys

  ❑ Follow-up on transactions

  ❑ Complaints

  ❑ Customer turnover and win/loss data

  ❑ Customer calls for service and inquiries

  ❑ Focus groups

- Understanding market requirements

- Understanding competitors and competitive offerings

- Strategic infrastructure support for front-line employees

- Focus on relationship management and enhancement

- High levels of customer satisfaction and customer awards

The Baldrige criteria further describes customer focus as impacting and integrating an organization's strategic directions, its value creation processes, and its business results. Chapter 3 describes the Malcolm Baldrige criteria in greater detail.

TOOLS/TECHNIQUES TO ASSESS THE STRENGTH OF A CUSTOMER-FOCUSED CULTURE

CEO Survey

In a recent survey, CEO's of multinational corporations identified becoming more customer-focused as a major challenge.[4] Therefore, it is necessary that a variety of strategic initiatives be examined and explored to help organizations face this challenge. Each technique and tool has its advantages and disadvantages, and based on its current culture and past experiences, an organization needs to adopt the best approach.

Malcolm Baldrige National Award Criteria

Probably the best tool to assess the strength of an organization's customer-focused culture is the Baldrige criteria.[5] This assessment tool will be discussed in subsequent chapters, but much of the emphasis of the Baldrige criteria is on alignment of approaches and actions with those things most important to customers. The Baldrige criteria provide a holistic view of the entire organization, beginning with leadership in Category 1 and ending with customer-related results in Category 7. Testimonials from those organizations that have been identified as leaders, as assessed by the Baldrige criteria, describe how the organizations were able to retain, gain or win back customers, revenue, and market share by implementing disciplined approaches focused on those things most important to customers.

A number of methods discussed in the next section of this chapter (Methods for Instituting and Reinforcing a Customer-Focused Culture) can be used to subjectively assess the strength of an organization's customer-focused culture. If pay increases are not being given because customer satisfaction or dissatisfaction results are not being achieved, then the methods being used may not be effective. It could also be that parts of the organization are still to employ the "customer first" concept. If employees cannot easily complete the sentences, "To help the organization achieve its customer satisfaction results, I will ...," they should be feeling fairly insecure about their contributions and future employment opportunities.

An organization needs to continuously look at the degree of importance of its goals. Is it financial performance, customer satisfaction, or something else? Each major performance review meeting should begin with the organization's showing customer satisfaction and/or dissatisfaction results. Executives should understand the direct correlation between customer satisfaction results and financial performance, or the adverse impact dissatisfaction has on financial results, including future revenue and current expenses. The correlation between customer-related data and financial performance is well-documented and has been discussed in detail in Appendix A. However, organizations seem hardpressed to believe another organization's results, so typically have to prove it to themselves using their own data. It does not matter what ever may be the type or size of an organization, there is a direct correlation between customer-related results and its financial performance.

A customer-focused organization constantly asks, "If I take this action, what impact will it have on customers"? An organization should be willing and eager to share ideas with its customers and get feedback. An important aspect in any supplier-customer relationship is the perceived value received. An organization should be able to explain to a customer the steps involved in producing the goods or services for which the customer is paying. If there is any doubt, it probably is a non-value added step that the customer does not recognize or would be willing to pay for. The assessment of value added process steps is usually conducted in an indirect way, without involving customers. If your organization does not include this assessment with every (major) decision that is made, then it is probably more internally focused than customer-focused. Customers provide the organization a plethora of information through a variety of methods such as complaints, inquiries, warranty returns, and survey results. An organization should be willing to share the results of the analysis conducted on such inputs from customers. This is akin to wearing a "customer-focused" brand. A newsletter is published twice a year by Johnson Controls, Inc., and distributed to customers stating the improvements that have been made as a result of customer input and feedback. This demonstrates that the organizations are listening to and acting on what they have been told.

Organizational Questions

To assess the strength of its customer-focused culture, an organization can conduct surveys of its employees. Survey questions may elicit responses that include:

- I understand the organization's commitment to customers
- I understand how my job and my actions are important to customers
- The organization places customers first

The most obvious indicator of an organization's commitment to a customer-focused culture is its customer-related information. This would include, but is not limited to, customer satisfaction results, complaint rates, market share rate, customer win/loss ratio, customer retention rate, and customer defection rate. All organizations have customers. Mostly, an organization has to work directly with its customers to define a set of customer-related indicators that best assess how well an organization is meeting customer expectations.

CREATING ORGANIZATIONAL STRUCTURES CONDUCIVE TO NURTURING A CUSTOMER-FOCUSED CULTURE

Complaint Management System

Organizations look for easy cures and quick fixes to its woes. Often, an organization creates new—or modifies existing—organizational structures in the hope this will solve internal problems or deficiencies. This technique tends to make things worse, because the accountability for an action or results does not shift with the realignment. Customer focus begins at the top of the organization. The leadership Category of the Baldrige criteria—the very first Category—asks how senior leaders in the organization set and deploy organization values, directions, and expectations focused on customers. Leaders need to be engaged, responsible, and held accountable for creating and demonstrating a customer-focused culture. A culture is not defined by how a firm is organized, it is defined by how employees at all levels of the organization behave.

The first thing an organization needs to be good at, if it hopes to become more customer-focused, is the handling of customer complaints. Complaints should be viewed as opportunities as opposed to burdens on the organization. This is not to say that more complaints are better, rather it indicates that customers are willing to give the organization a chance to address their concerns as opposed to asking someone else (e.g., your competitor) to address them. Since the handling of complaints is paramount to effective customer satisfaction results and ongoing relationships, those handling complaints should be well trained on how to deal with and defuse rough situations. They should be empowered to resolve issues on the spot. One measurement of effective complaint handling is the percentage of complaints resolved within the initial contact by the customer. Since this is such an important aspect for the organization, a separate department should be set up to deal with complaints, track them, and manage them to resolution. This department should report to a senior executive within the organization, and the results and issues should be reviewed by the senior management on a regular basis.

Customer Support Organization

Once an effective complaint management process and department have been established, the organization needs to put in place another department to gather, analyze, measure and manage customer satisfaction information. Typically, this means conducting customer satisfaction surveys that may be contracted to an outside firm. There are a number of methods of conducting customer satisfaction surveys. A good reference book for this purpose is 'Customer Centered Six Sigma: Linking Customers, Process Improvement, and Financial Results, by Earl Naumann and Steven H. Hoisington, published by ASQ Quality Press, Milwaukee, Wisconsin, USA, 2001. The process of gathering customer satisfaction survey data will invariably result in some findings of dissatisfaction. Without an effective complaint management process, efforts to survey customers will only make them more dissatisfied if no action is taken to address their concerns. The customer satisfaction management department must be empowered to get the organization to take action on the results of the survey. It may be responsible for setting the measurement and goals that impact the organization's variable pay system (discussed in the next section of this chapter). The department should report to a senior executive in the organization, and the results and issues should be reviewed by the senior management on a regular basis.

The first two steps assume an organization has already been in existence, with predefined customers and markets. An organization needs to first identify the needs, requirements, and expectations of customers in order to develop and produce goods and services that meet these. A department devoted to market, customer, or industry research needs to be in place to understand new and changing requirements. This will assist the organization in proactively addressing the internal and external factors affecting an organization [illustrated in Figure 1.1]. To be effective, the research department needs to collaborate with the complaint management department as well as the customer satisfaction management team. In most organizations, this group reports to the senior executive responsible for sales and marketing or to the senior executive responsible for product/service development.

There are a number of methods used to organize people and departments in a firm, many unique in their approach. The Conference Board provides examples of structures for hundreds of organizations—with no two being completely alike.[6] Each structure has its advantages and disadvantages. In the opinion of the authors, an organizational structure that supports what is most important to customers is most effective. The next section of this chapter discusses the alignment of processes and internal measurements with those things most important to customers. Ideally, an organization should align itself to support this structure. In other words, processes to support customer requirements should be identified, and then work units (departments) should be formed to manage and own these processes. A senior executive should be assigned ownership to each of these major processes. This prevents an organization from being focused or aligned by vertical, functionally oriented silos.

INTEGRATE CUSTOMER-FOCUSED ATTRIBUTES INTO ALL JOB DESCRIPTIONS

Employees in the organization should be organized in such a way that they support key customer requirements. Every employee should be asked, and should be able to answer the following questions:

- Who are your customers?
- What are their requirements?
- What are the key issues impacting customers today?
- How does your work affect customer satisfaction or dissatisfaction results or outcomes?
- What actions are you responsible for in helping the organization achieve customer satisfaction results?

Once again, a culture is not defined by how a firm is organized, it is defined by the behavior of the employees at all levels of the organization.

METHODS FOR INSTITUTING AND REINFORCING A CUSTOMER-FOCUSED CULTURE

Vision, Mission, Objectives That Include Customer Focus

As mentioned earlier, the Baldrige criteria describes a customer-focused culture as one that impacts and integrates an organization's strategic directions, its value creation processes, and its business results. Therefore, it only makes sense that an organization create and implement approaches and rewards that support these factors. To begin with, an organization needs to develop a policy, vision, or mission that supports a customer-focused environment. For instance, IBM Rochester, winner of the Malcolm Baldrige National Quality Award in 1990, created a vision that read, "Become the undisputed worldwide leader in customer satisfaction." The mission statement at Johnson Controls, Inc., reads, "Continually exceed our customer's increasing expectations." One of the five values at Johnson Controls, Inc., is customer satisfaction. As mentioned earlier, the leadership Category of the Baldrige criteria asks how senior leaders in the organization set and deploy organization values, directions and expectations focused on customers, among other things.

Incentive Pay

A reward and recognition system helps reinforce desired behaviors. If a focus on customers is important, then employees should be rewarded accordingly. A measurement system needs to be established to support the desired behavior of "being customer focused." Typically, these measurements include customer satisfaction scores, reduction in the number or percentage of customer complaints, customer retention rates, customer loyalty rates and percentage of new customers acquired. In several organizations, a part of the employee's pay or bonus is tied to any or all of these measurements. For instance, at IBM, 15 percent of employee variable pay was contingent on achieving aggressive customer satisfaction survey results for the year. At Johnson Controls, Inc., up to 20 percent of an executive's variable compensation is dependent upon achievement of customer satisfaction results, survey completion rate, and complaint arrival rate.

It is also important to reinforce focus on customers through an organization's performance management system. At IBM, the performance plan for every individual begins with the statement, "In order to help the organization achieve its customer satisfaction results, I will . . .." This helps individuals identify ways to be personally involved in helping the organization achieve its desired objectives. A manager should be able to ask an employee to identify the customer, their requirements and expectations, current issues, and the actions being taken to improve customer satisfaction.

Value Models

A technique that world-class organizations use to provide a focus on customers and to align resources to support this is to align processes that support customer requirements. The first step in this technique is to define the elements most important to customers. These are called value models. Every value model contains six major elements[7]:

- Product quality
- Service quality
- Relationship
- Delivery
- Price
- Image

Figure 1.3 depicts a customer view model developed by IBM Rochester.[8] Based on customer input, 43 specific attributes were identified and grouped into six major categories: technical solutions (hardware and software quality), maintenance and service support (hardware and software service), marketing/sales offerings, administration, delivery, and image. Recognizing that these six major categories and 43 attributes are the principal drivers of overall customer satisfaction, IBM Rochester then determined the processes that impacted these attributes. Figure 1.4 shows the alignment of the customer view model, processes, and internal measurements of IBM Rochester. It is important to understand the alignment of customer needs and expectations with internal processes. For instance, IBM Rochester previously focused quite heavily on the "manufacturing" process, but customers stated that they did not view IBM Rochester

IBM Rochester—Customer View Model

Customer View of IBM AS/400 Product

Customer Satisfaction Measurements

Overall Satisfaction, Loyalty, Recommend

Common Attributes

Ease of doing-business with • Partnership • Responsiveness • Knowledge of customer's business • Customer driven

Major Categories	Technical Solutions		Maintenance and Service Support		Marketing/Sales Offerings		Administration	Delivery	Image
Customer Attributes	Hardware	Software	Hardware Service	Software Service	Channel	Sales Person			
	Quality/Reliability		Single Contact Point		Central Contact Point		Purchasing Procedure	On time	Corporate Citizen
	Availability		Flexible		Information		Billing Procedure	Without Defects	Community Interests
	Ease of Use		Available		Solution Provider		Terms and Conditions	To Specification	Social Concerns
	Disaster Recovery Process		Product Knowledge		Product Knowledge		Warranty Expiration Notification	Post Delivery Process	Environment Consciousness
	Documentation		Accessible		Education		Financial Alternatives	Accurate	Technology Leader
	Openness		Empowered		Empowered				Financial Stability
	Growth				Competent				Executives' Image
	Price/Pricing				Ethical				Empathy
	Warranty								
	New Technology								
	Installation/Upgradability								

Fig. 1.3 IBM Rochester Customer View Model (Six Major Categories, 43 Attributes)

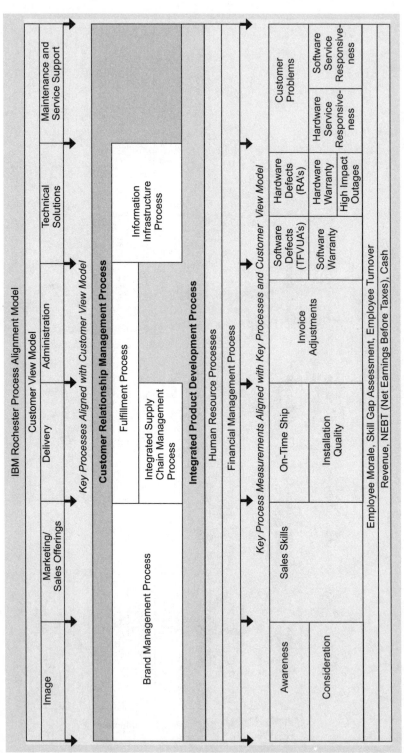

Fig. 1.4 Alignment of IBM Rochester Customer View Model Attributes with Key Processes and Key Process Measurement

as having a "manufacturing" process, but rather a fulfillment process. Customers stated that they placed an order for a product, and the product was delivered. What happened in between was irrelevant to them unless it caused the product to be shipped defective or late. Therefore, IBM Rochester expanded its overall fulfillment process to include the ordering sub-process, the sub-process used to hand-off the order to the manufacturing process, and the delivery sub-process. When the organization can link customer needs, expectations and requirements to its processes, the process can be redesigned to improve not only the financial performance of the company but customer satisfaction as well. It is against the customer's expectations that process performance will eventually be evaluated.

Examples of value models for AT&T (Figure 1.5) and Johnson Controls, Inc. (Figures 1.6 and 1.7) are also shown.[9] In each case, these organizations determined the key requirements of customers, developed processes aligned with—and in support of—these requirements, and systematically determined internal measurements to assess performance.

SUMMARY

To remain competitive and in existence, most organizations have little choice when it comes to becoming [more] customer focused. A number of internal and external factors impact an organization on a regular basis, all competing for resources or forcing the organization to change. There is a direct correlation between the strength of an organization's customer-focused culture and its financial performance. Organizational Leaders and CEO's have identified the need to become customer-focused as a key challenge for many multinational organizations. Becoming a customer-focused organization begins with senior leaders setting the direction and "walking the talk." An organization that is customer focused places the customer first, aligns its processes to support customers, and holds everyone in the organization accountable for achieving customer satisfaction results. There are a number of tools and techniques an organization can use to assess the strength of its customer-focused culture. The Baldrige criteria provide the most comprehensive view of an organization's customer-focused culture. Organizations look for ways to reorganize in order to become more customer-focused. Developing customer support processes and teams are important, as is alignment of resources and processes to directly support customer requirements. However, a culture is not

AT&T Value Model

Business Process	Customer Need/Expectation		Internal Metric
30% Product	Reliability	40%	# of Repair Calls
	Easy to Use	20%	# of Calls for Help
	Features/Functions	40%	Functional Performance Test
	Knowledge	30%	Supervisor Observations
20% Sales	Responsive	25%	% Proposal Made on Time
	Follow-Up	10%	% Follow-Up Made
	Delivery Interval Meet Needs	30%	Average Order Interval
15% Installation	Does Not Break	25%	% Repair Reports
	Installed When Promised	10%	% Installed on Due Date
	No Repeat Trouble	30%	% Repeat Reports
15% Repair	Fixed Fast	25%	Average Speed of Repair
	Kept Informed	10%	% Customers Informed
15% Billing	Accuracy, No Surprise	45%	% Billing Inquiries
	Resolved on First Call	35%	% Resolved First Calls
	Easy to Understand	10%	% Billing Inquiries

Overall Product and Service Quality

Fig. 1.5 AT&T Value Model with Internal Metrics

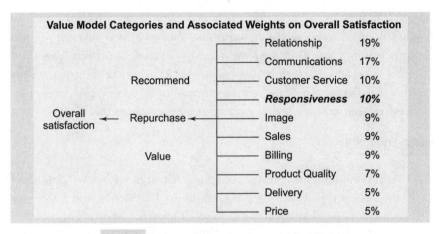

Value Model Categories and Associated Weights on Overall Satisfaction

	Relationship	19%
	Communications	17%
Recommend	Customer Service	10%
	Responsiveness	*10%*
Overall satisfaction ← Repurchase ←	Image	9%
	Sales	9%
Value	Billing	9%
	Product Quality	7%
	Delivery	5%
	Price	5%

Fig. 1.6   Johnson Controls, Inc., Value Model

Responsiveness

Survey Question	Business Process
IQ33: Committing resources	■ Planning and scheduling ■ Customer communication ■ Sales forecast ■ Hiring ■ Training ■ Certification
IQ28: Promptly addressing questions	■ Call escalation ■ Bid-submittal ■ Project management/tools ■ Escalation process ■ Introductory letter
SQ43: Resolve problems on one visit	■ Dispatching ■ Technical training ■ Cross training ■ Certification ■ Account management plan
Q11: Fast accurate two-way communication	■ Utilize Nextel system or equivalent ■ Dispatching ■ Kick-off meeting ■ Turnover
SQ41: Quick emergency response	■ Call escalation ■ Service dispatch/administration ■ Account management

Fig. 1.7   Alignment of Customer Requirements, Processes, and Internal Measurements at Johnson Controls, Inc.

defined by how a firm is organized, it is defined by the behavior of all the employees at all levels of the organization. Therefore, it is necessary to put approaches in place that reinforce desired behaviors, especially those that support a customer-focused environment and help achieve desired customer satisfaction results. The most common methods used to reinforce a customer-focused environment are the recognition and reward programs.

REFERENCES

(1) Earl Naumann and Steve Hoisington, "Customer Loyalty," published in proceedings from the ASQ's Business Excellence and Customer Satisfaction Conference, New Orleans, Louisiana, USA, 9—11 February 2002.

(2) Earl Naumann and Steven H. Hoisington, "Customer Centered Six Sigma: Linking Customers, Process Improvement, and Financial Results," published by ASQ Quality Press, Milwaukee, Wisconsin, USA, 2001.

(3) Malcolm Baldrige National Quality Award, United States Department of Commerce, United States Department of Commerce, Technology Administration, National Institute of Standards and Technology, Baldrige National Quality Award Program, Administration Building, Room A635, 100 Bureau Drive, Stop 1020, Gaithersburg, Maryland, 20899-1020, USA. http://www.nist.gov.

(4) David Dell, Ph.D, "The CEO Challenge: Top Marketplace and Management Issues-2002," The Conference Board, 845 Third Avenue, New York, NY 10022-6679, USA, 2002.

(5) Malcolm Baldrige National Quality Award, United States Department of Commerce, United States Department of Commerce, Technology Administration, National Institute of Standards and Technology, Baldrige National Quality Award Program, Administration Building, Room A635, 100 Bureau Drive, Stop 1020, Gaithersburg, Maryland, 20899-1020, USA. http://www.nist.gov.

(6) The Conference Board, 845 Third Avenue, New York, NY 10022-6679, USA (212) 759–0900.

(7) Steve Hoisington and Earl Naumann, "The Loyalty Elephant," published in Quality Progress Magazine by ASQ Quality Press, Milwaukee, Wisconsin, USA, February 2003.

(8) Earl Naumann and Steven H. Hoisington, "Customer Centered Six Sigma: Linking Customers, Process Improvement, and Financial Results," published by ASQ Quality Press, Milwaukee, Wisconsin, USA, 2001.

(9) Ibid.

LEVERAGING STRATEGIES FOR CREATING STAKEHOLDER VALUE

IMPLEMENTING A FLEXIBLE AND AGILE STRATEGIC PLANNING FRAMEWORK

Businesses or organizations exist to serve customers. Without customers, there is no purpose or meaning for any organization. We all have customers. Creation of shareholder value or stakeholder value, in a more broader sense, is how businesses or organizations continue to exist. However, the route or approaches adopted by most organizations to reach their end goals often vary and that is understandable. There is no one proven method that will help any organization successfully achieve its goals. The best organizations have figured this out and apply the best methods to each unique situation. The difficulty faced by many organizations has been to quantify shareholder or stakeholder value and get the rest of the organization to accept it as a means to drive the business planning process.

Typically, in most organizations, the focus of business plans is to place great emphasis on operational budgets, with the aim to be competitively superior in financial measures such as higher gross margins, return on investment (ROI) and so forth. Experience shows that this approach pays dividends in the short term, but, perhaps, falls short over the longer term. This is a reactionary approach as opposed to a strategic one. A recipe for sustained success both in the short and longer term is what is needed for modern day businesses and organizations. A balanced business plan that supports the organization from a short and longer term strategic perspective can be described by the three pillars of success. These pillars, as illustrated in Figure 2.1, are strategy, measures, and value. Each of these pillars is explained in detail in the following sections.

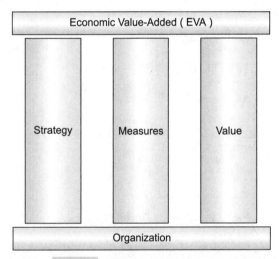

Fig. 2.1 EVA and the Three Pillars

Pillar 1—Strategy and Strategic Planning

Central to the success of any organization is a need to have a strong foundation for a robust strategic planning process. The Malcolm Baldrige National Quality Award criteria, referred to in Chapter 1, devote an entire category (Category 2) to Strategic Planning.[1] Item 2.1 deals with Strategy Development and Item 2.2 deals with Strategy Deployment. The overarching theme that is suggested of an organization, based upon the Baldrige criteria for Category 2, is an integrated and aligned approach to the organization's purpose, vision, mission, plans, goals, objectives, action plans, and resources. This is depicted in Figure 2.2. Additionally, details regarding the Malcolm Baldrige National Quality Award criteria will be explained in Chapter 3.

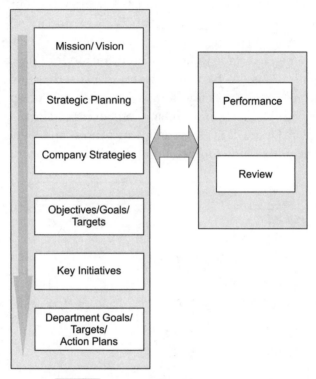

Fig. 2.2 Strategy-Driven Performance

The key outcome of a strategic development process is a set of strategies which should, when deployed efficiently and effectively, allow the organization to deliver on shareholder or stakeholder value, guarantee sustained performance of the organization, and allow the organization to outperform the competition and give it the desired market leadership position. In arriving at those strategies, the organization needs to factor in data pertaining to current and future customers, competition, organizational capability, and capability and skill sets of its work force, among other factors.

Strategy Development

A typical strategic planning process, as depicted in Figure 2.3, would consist of the following steps:

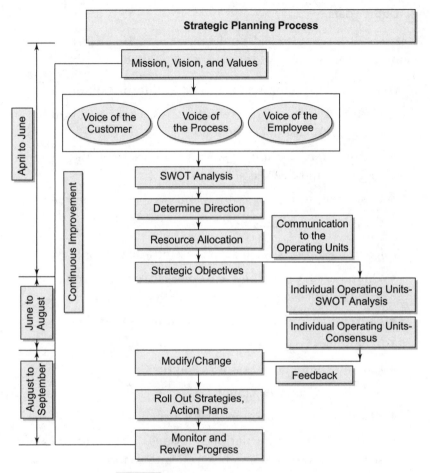

Fig. 2.3 Strategic Planning Process

1. Review and revisit of the mission, vision and values

Any planning process needs to begin with a review of the current vision, mission, and values of the organization. This is a necessary step in order to check and verify its relevance with regard to the current state of the organization. It is good to start from the vision statement—the "to be" state of the organization, and then work on tweaking the mission, or what the organization delivers to its shareholders.

2. Gather data

A variety of inputs, backed by data, needs to be factored into the planning process. Some of those inputs could be:

a. Voice of the Customer, such as data or information on:

- Customer expectations/requirements, segmented by different market and customer segments
- Competition, including specifics in each of the customer segments and markets
- Customer satisfaction, overall and on specific requirements
- Customer complaints

b. Voice of the Process, such as data or information on:

- Operational capabilities covering all existing business and support processes
- Current performance levels of all those processes
- Technology road maps
- Capital equipment or Capex requirements
- Supplier/partner capabilities
- Regulatory and environmental issues
- National and international issues including local tax structures, ways of doing business, and so forth

c. Voice of the Employee, such as data and information on:

- Current employee retention and attrition rates
- Employee satisfaction, including satisfaction segmented by different levels
- Safety or injury incident rates
- Employee absenteeism rates
- Employee headcount and skill requirements

3. SWOT analysis

With all relevant information now available, it is useful to conduct a detailed analysis on the organization's strengths, weaknesses, opportunities, and threats (SWOT). This is normally carried out at the level of the senior leadership, with appropriate representation from different levels of management, including labor unions, key customers, key partners, and suppliers. Many organizations have a person or function devoted to determining SWOT analysis characteristics, constantly monitoring the industry, market, competitors, and new, emerging, or changing requirements.

4. Determine direction

At this point in time, the organization should be in a position to articulate its long-term and annual plans in line with its vision. Short- and long-term horizons may vary depending on the industry. There is no standard for any organization. For example, long term for the software industry is perhaps less than two years, for telecom less than three years, and five years for major space projects/defense contractors. Annual strategic objectives can now be derived from the long-range plans.

5. Allocate resources including staffing plans

To deliver on the agreed strategic objectives, careful thought needs to be given to the issue of resources. Resources could be in the form of staffing plans, skill requirements, and basic infrastructure such as IT systems. It is essential to link human resource plans with the organization's overall business plans. A simple method depicting this integration and alignment is shown in Figure 2.4. In Column 1, the current headcount information for each of the major departments or divisions is indicated. The head of each department is then asked to indicate headcount projections for the next four quarters, in line with the business goals or the strategic objectives. Aggregation of those inputs will result in a consolidated picture relative to the headcount at the organizational level. Usually, the head of Human Resources in concert with the Chief of Finance will then indicate the affordable headcount based on projected levels of profitability for the next fiscal year. A very similar exercise is carried out to determine capital equipment or Capex requirements and other overhead expenses such as telephones, copiers, IT systems, and so forth. A report generated every quarter helps track actual performance to what was planned.

Current Headcount as of 9/30/XX for each Department	Projection for FY XX				Headcount End FY XX
	1st Quarter	2nd Quarter	3rd Quarter	4th Quarter	
Officers #					
Executives #					
Managers #					
Associates #					
Others #					
Total #					

Current list of Capital Equipment as of 9/30/XX for each Department	Projection for FY XX				Headcount End FY XX
	1st Quarter	2nd Quarter	3rd Quarter	4th Quarter	
Total #					

Current Position of Overhead as of 9/30/XX for each Department (Telephones, Copiers, System)	Projection for FY XX				Headcount End FY XX
	1st Quarter	2nd Quarter	3rd Quarter	4th Quarter	
Total #					

Fig. 2.4 Template for Resource Allocations

6. Communicate and obtain feedback

At this stage, the complete set of strategic objectives, along with action plans and individual requirements to assign accountability, that has been determined by the senior leadership team is now shared with the rest of the organization through appropriate levels of management. It is necessary to get the buy-in of everyone in the organization to ensure alignment and to increase the chances of success in meeting planned objectives. There are various methods that can be used to align department and individual performance goals in support of the organization's strategic objectives, goals, and action plans. One example is the use of Hoshin Planning.[2] This method will be discussed in detail in Chapter 9. An example of this method employed by Johnson Controls, Inc., is depicted in Figures 9.2A, 9.2B, and 9.2C.

7. Modify and change based on feedback

The individual operating units need to review what is being asked of them in order to help the organization as a whole achieve its plans and objectives. These units may need to do their own SWOT analysis to determine the feasibility of delivering on the expectations. Once all such inputs have been received from all the operating units, an aggregation of agreed upon strategies, action plans and expectations is possible.

8. Rollout strategies and action plans with assigned accountability

The finalized set of strategies—both short and long term—along with action plans and measurable objectives can now be rolled out across the organization. Accountability needs to be assigned to department heads, process owners, individuals, and suppliers and partners as appropriate.

9. Monitor and review progress

A regular set of reviews and reports is required to track, monitor and review progress on action plans and objectives. This should be done at the highest level in the organization (e.g. corporate reviews), as well as cascaded to all lower levels where accountability has been assigned. The old adage "What gets measured, monitored and reviewed gets improved" applies here. From a strategic perspective, it is important to monitor overall performance at least quarterly, but in some cases, monthly monitoring, especially for industries with short product life cycles, may be in order. Category 1 of the Baldrige criteria discusses the need for organization-wide performance reviews by senior management and the need to provide assistance to individuals or functions that are not meeting expectations.[3]

10. Evaluate and improve the planning process

Evaluation and improvement of processes should be conducted regularly in all organizations. Evaluation and improvement of the planning process is critical since this drives the overall direction of the organization, leading to deliverance of customer value and attainment of overall goals. Improvements to the planning process can benefit from a variety of inputs including key supplier and customer involvement in the planning process, and working on key accountability for the board members in an organization (company) such that they are active participants and key contributors to the development of the strategies, action plans, and objectives. Assignment of accountability to board members will be discussed in more detail in Chapter 10 (Board Governance).

Strategy Deployment

As has been noted earlier, strategies need to be deployed across the organization and tracked for performance. There is a need, therefore, to build a set of measures that are mapped to the strategies, that result in a performance measurement system that the organization can use to track progress on an ongoing basis. Typically, as discussed in the beginning of this chapter, the measures that an organization tends to focus on are operational numbers or financial measures such as the gross margin or ROI. However, for a robust strategic management system, the key is to have a combination of financial and non-financial measures. Non-financial measures, to name a few, could be customer satisfaction, employee satisfaction and productivity. It is this combination of measures that helps organizations achieve two things:

1. Address the needs of its stakeholder community, facilitated by those strategies, and

2. Monitor the progress relative to the realization of those strategies through a measurement system that has both financial and non-financial measures.

Such a combination of measures is sometimes referred to as the Balanced Scorecard. Harvard Business School professor Robert Kaplan and management consultant David Norton conceived the Balanced Scorecard in 1991. First introduced in a 1992 *Harvard Business Review* article, it was further followed up by seminal work in 1993 and 1996. The landmark book, *The Balanced Scorecard: Translating Strategy into Action*, was published in 1996[4]. Additional information regarding the Balanced Scorecard has been discussed in Chapter 6.

Pillar 2—Measures: Linking Balanced Scorecard and Strategy

Kaplan and Norton followed up their initial book with another one a few years later—*The Strategy Focused Organization.* In this book, they built on the initial work and came out with the concept of strategy maps.[5] Chapter 6 discusses in detail the relevance of strategy maps and their use in implementing a scorecard in a company. The focus of their book is to look at the strategic objectives derived from the organization's strategy in four different perspectives—financial, customer, internal processes, and learning and growth. Interpreted differently, if we now work on the measures that map into those strategic objectives, we will have a mix of financial and non-financial measures that were discussed in the previous section.

Another key concept, the authors emphasize, is the importance of developing a cause-and-effect relationship between the strategic objectives that result from the development of strategy maps. This facilitates the organization to arrive at measures—both leading and lagging—to make those strategic objectives work. In other words, since strategy is central to the development of the scorecard, one can refer to it as a "Strategic Measurement System" or a "Strategic Management System."

Pillar 3—Value: Integrating the EVA Principles into Key Business Strategies

What Is EVA

EVA or Economic Value-Added is one single metric that measures the overall success of the organization. EVA measures the wealth of the organization and, hence, is a direct indicator of shareholder value. EVA, by definition, is net operating profit after tax (NOPAT) minus the capital charge. First introduced by Stern and Stewart, "creating sustainable improvements in EVA is synonymous with increasing shareholder wealth".[6] In simpler terms, in the parlance of the current accounting practices, the profit declared by organizations is usually what remains after deducting taxes from the net operating profits. EVA goes a step further. Protagonists of EVA submit to the fact that those profits—the money left to service equity—is not profit. Until a business returns a profit that is greater than its cost of capital, it is operating at a loss. Arithmetically, it is after tax operating profits minus the appropriate capital charge for both debt and equity.

Linking Strategy, Balanced Scorecard and EVA

Tangible versus Intangible

The genesis of the Balanced Scorecard approach took its roots in the recognition of the value of the distinction between tangible and intangible assets. In any organization tangible assets are more visible. They are the physical assets such as machinery and capital equipment that often end up with a specific value in the balance sheet of the organization. They are a key component in the determination of the financial returns of the organization. On the other hand, intangible or invisible assets have to do with how well the organization performs in its execution at customer relationship management, motivated and empowered workforce, high quality products or services, less time to market products and services, and best in class internal processes.

The value add in the Balanced Scorecard concept is the consideration of these intangible or intellectual assets through measurements or measures that could complement the conventional measures such as ROI, asset utilization, profits, and so forth. The combination of financial and non-financial measures provides the necessary balance to complement each other and a robust enough scorecard which, if implemented properly, could be a recipe for sustained market leadership.

Recipe for Success—Short versus Long-Term

Conventional business practices, in the realm of corporate governance have leaned more toward judging the performance of the organization on financial parameters such as earnings per share, ROI, gross margins, overall revenue, profit after tax, and so forth. Corporate board meetings are invariably focused on financial results and deciding the amount of dividends to be paid out to the shareholders.

The shift to judging an organization's performance on both financial and non-financial criteria is a recent phenomenon. Organizations in this space are beginning to realize that they stand to gain much more with this approach. Non-financial parameters such as customer loyalty index, on-time delivery, employee satisfaction, and productivity per employee are some of the measurements that merit mention as possible candidates that need to complement the financial ones to create the much needed balance in developing an organization scorecard. Appendix A discusses the correlation of financial and non-financial measurements at IBM Rochester as an example where focusing on non-financial measurements is just as important as focusing on the financial ones.[7]

The intangible measures discussed in the previous section address the needs and expectations of the important stakeholders such as customers, employees and community. Over the longer term, it is this focus on key stakeholders and intangible measures that ensures an organization's success. The financial focus tends to be more myopic. Therefore, it is a combination of financial and non-financial measurements that lead to sustained performance over the long term. Recent surveys of the top executives of Fortune 500 companies reveal that many consider non-financial parameters as being important, although opinion is divided on their use to measure and actually drive improvements.[8] But the shift in thinking is perceptible in many organizations, some driven by stakeholder input.

Economic Fundamentals of Value-Based Management

As stated in the beginning of this chapter, the goal of all organizations is to maximize "value-added" to the key resources employed.[9] In sectors such as IT, media and entertainment, and fast moving consumer goods (FMCG), intangible capital such as human capital, brands, and patents are key resources and far more valuable than traditional financial capital, even though they may not show up adequately on financial statements. However, the key economic fundamentals of shareowner value-based management in these industries are the same as in any other sector. Figure 2.5 illustrates examples of the economic fundamentals of value-based management.

Economic fundamentals of value-based management	Why these fundamentals are important in industries with high intangible capital
1. Cash flow economics drive sustainable shareowner value	Intangible capital is a huge reservoir of potential that needs to be tapped and leveraged before the competitive advantage lapses
2. Managers must manage both for the short term and the long term	Investors future growth expectation of the value they invest is a given. Therefore, to create lasting shareowner wealth, managers need to simultaneously convert potential into actual performance (short term) and be cognizant to work that value into the future (long term)
3. Organization economics represent a difficult trade-off between coordination and motivation	Knowledge-intensive businesses cannot thrive in great bureaucracies. To deliver on the growth expectation, they require empowerment and decentralization to cope with changing environment (e.g., customer needs, technology shifts, competitor moves, etc.). Hence, the organizational design must allow for decentralization, coupled with sufficient accountability, motivation, and the attendant incentives to ensure value creation

Fig. 2.5   Economic Fundamentals of Value-Based Management

Key Principles of the EVA Framework

Figure 2.6 captures the key principles of the EVA framework and how organizations can incorporate them to better manage value

Key principles of the EVA framework	How organizations can incorporate them to better manage value creation
1. What gets measured gets managed	1. Identify performance measures— financial and non-financial—tied to the business goals or to the strategic objectives 2. Systematically aligned to the shareowner wealth creation but not prone to the vagaries of capital markets
2. Empowerment, decentralization, and accountability	1. Identify the people accountable for short-term and long-term components of value creation 2. Identify and hold them accountable for value drivers (measures)
3. You get what you pay for—so align the interests of employees with those of shareowners to sustain long-term performance	Develop performance-linked variable incentives that are: 1. significant and relative to fixed pay 2. not tied to annual budgets, but tie targets to long-term shareowner expectations 3. matching the payout mode with the time frame of value creation (e.g., short term and long term) as appropriate

Fig. 2.6 Key Principles of the EVA Framework

creation. The main point here is to consider EVA as the overarching financial goal and work on a mechanism to cascade and align that goal to applicable work centers. In essence, that means:

- to identify performance measures (financial and non-financial) that are tied to the business goals, and

- to identify the people accountable for the short-term and long-term components of the value creation

Integrating BSC and EVA

From the discussion so far, it is clear that both the Balanced Scorecard (BSC) and Economic Value-Added (EVA) point to or favor positioning of financial and non-financial dimensions in a way that they are complementary to each other. In order to effectively integrate BSC into the EVA framework, the following are required:

- First, introduce a hierarchy into the four scorecard perspectives with shareowner value creation as the overarching objective. Organizations should use improvements in EVA at the apex of its financial measures to prioritize objectives that are cascaded throughout the organization for short-term success.

- Second, explicitly identify strategies, action plans, and leading indicators to create shareowner value for the longer term.

EVA drivers are a set of diagnostic tools that trace the creation of EVA to individual financial and non-financial performance variables and help the managers in an organization to maintain a clear and sharp focus. However, most employees do not have a direct impact on the organization's EVA: a simple EVA calculation is too vague a guide for day-to-day actions. Employees have control over key measures that ultimately impact EVA. The linkage of strategies, the corresponding measures and EVA is shown in Figure 2.7.

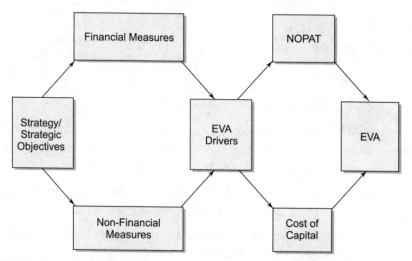

Fig. 2.7 Linkage of Strategy, Measures (Financial and Non-financial), and EVA

Figure 2.8 shows an example of the use of this concept in an IT company. The measures depict a combination of financial (e.g. revenue, Weighted Average Cost of Capital (WACC), etc.) and non-financial (customer loyalty index, ROI on training, etc.), parameters which, in turn, drive net operating profit after tax (NOPAT) and cost of capital, respectively, to generate the EVA. And finally, Figure 2.9 shows the manner in which measures can be mapped into the four-perspective scorecard that drives implementation of EVA. Therefore,

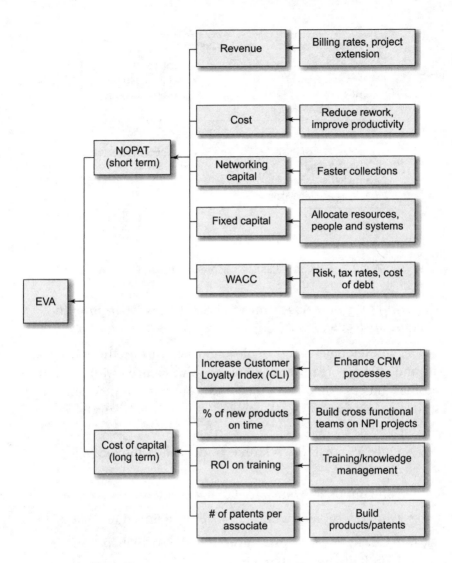

Fig. 2.8 Value Drivers (Measures) for an IT Business

just like for any other project, the Balanced Scorecard needs to be done in a project management environment. And in much the same manner as any other activities or initiatives, senior leadership commitment, buy-in and support are key ingredients for the success of this project. Chapter 6 covers, in detail, the implementation of the Balanced Scorecard and Chapter 10 discusses the use of EVA to judge organizational performance as part of corporate governance.

Internal Process	Customer
• Productivity • Project Planning • Recruitment • Resource Allocation	• Response Time • On Time Delivery • Domain Expertise
Financial	**Learning and Growth**
• Rate/License Price • Billable Hours • Receivables • Sales and Marketing	• Continuous Education • Right Skills

Drives EVA

Fig. 2.9   EVA and Balanced Scorecard for an IT Business

Ensuring Ongoing Assessment of Strategies to Align with Changing Needs

Strategy development and deployment need to be the focal point around which organizations must rally. Hence, with changing business needs, there is a need to constantly review and align strategies. A recent Chief Financial Officer (CFO) survey revealed the following[10]:

- Only 5% of the workforce understands the strategy of the company

- Nine out of 20 companies fail to execute strategy

- Only 25% of managers have incentives linked to strategy

- As many as 85% executives spend less than one hour per month discussing strategy

- As many as 60% of organizations don't link budgets to strategy

As is explained in Chapter 6, most companies start with due diligence to develop a first-cut set of strategies at the beginning of each planning cycle. However, more often than not, they develop a tendency to focus on operational numbers and targets in most of the quarterly reviews, and, therefore, lose focus on the strategies per se. It is equally important to keep under active consideration the long-term business strategies and be sensitive to changes, as environments and market conditions change, and factor the changes in the short-term strategies and the corresponding operational plans. Strategy development and deployment are dynamic entities that serve as barometers from which the fortunes and success of organizations are derived. Additionally, agility in responding to rapid changes in the market place and fine-tuning strategy to the changing environment are also very important. No organization can rest on a "one-off" strategy that is no longer relevant in a changed environment, market place, or industry. Chapter 5 discusses the aspects of change and change management processes in greater detail.

SUMMARY

All organizations exist to serve its customers. Creation of shareholder value or wealth is the reason why most organizations continue to exist. Economic Value-Added or EVA is a workable and a catch-all methodology that can help measure and generate wealth, provided it is well understood and implemented. The key to that outcome is centered around the consideration of financial and non-financial measures that act as value drivers which ultimately ensures long-term success. The shift in corporate governance, from focusing on just the financial measures, to both financial and non-financial measures, is a trend that organizations are beginning to explore. Although there are a number of competing methodologies, similarities exist between EVA and the Balanced Scorecard (BSC) and how these methods complement each other to provide a recipe for organizational success.

REFERENCES

(1) Malcolm Baldrige National Quality Award, United States Department of Commerce, United States Department of Commerce, Technology Administration, National Institute of Standards and Technology, Baldrige National Quality Award Program, Administration Building, Room A635, 100 Bureau Drive, Stop 1020, Gaithersburg, Maryland, 20899–1020, USA. http://www.nist.gov.

(2) Earl Naumann and Steven H. Hoisington, "Customer Centered Six Sigma: Linking Customers, Process Improvement, and Financial Results," published by ASQ Quality Press, Milwaukee, Wisconsin, USA, 2001.

(3) Malcolm Baldrige National Quality Award, United States Department of Commerce, United States Department of Commerce, Technology

Administration, National Institute of Standards and Technology, Baldrige National Quality Award Program, Administration Building, Room A635, 100 Bureau Drive, Stop 1020, Gaithersburg, Maryland, 20899–1020, USA. http://www.nist.gov.

(4) Robert S. Kaplan and David P. Norton, "Translating Strategy into action—The Balanced Scorecard," Harvard Business School Press, Boston, Massachusetts, USA, 1996.

(5) Robert S. Kaplan and David P. Norton, "The Strategy Focused Organization—How Balanced Scorecard Companies Thrive in the New Business Environment," Harvard Business School Press, Boston, Massachusetts, USA, 2001.

(6) Joel M. Stern and John. S. Shiely, "The EVA Challenge— Implementing Value Added Change in an Organization," John Wiley and Sons, New York, NY, USA, December 12, 2003.

(7) Earl Naumann and Steven H. Hoisington, "Customer Centered Six Sigma: Linking Customers, Process Improvement, and Financial Results," published by ASQ Quality Press, Milwaukee, Wisconsin, USA, 2001.

(8) Ester V. Rudis, "The CEO Challenge 2003: Top Marketplace and Management Issues," The Conference Board, 845 Third Avenue, New York, NY, 10022–6679, USA, 2003.

(9) Tejpavan Gandhok and Sanjay Kulkarni, "EVAluation–Intangible Value Added", Harvard Business Review, Volume 4, Issue 1, Boston, Massachusetts, USA, January 2002.

(10) "SAP—Strategic Enterprise Management—Translating Strategy into Action"; The Balanced Scorecard; David Norton. The Balanced Scorecard Collaborative, Inc., and by SEM Product Management, SAP AG, Neurostrasse 16.69190 Walldorf, Germany, May 1999.

CHAPTER THREE

ASSESSING ORGANIZATIONAL CAPABILITIES—THE BALDRIGE MODEL

All organizations, no matter their size or type, need to assess their capabilities in order to determine key strengths and areas for improvement or opportunities. Sometimes, this is not a voluntary effort and may be brought on when an organization is struggling to survive. This chapter will discuss a few different methods an organization could use to assess its performance and capabilities. Based on years of experience, working with organizations around the world and using different assessment models, the authors believe that the assessment models presented in this chapter look at an organization in a holistic manner. They are some of the best models, but not the only ones. The authors believe that the Malcolm Baldrige National Quality Award Criteria for Performance Excellence model is the premier assessment tool in place today. Therefore, it will receive more attention in the discussion throughout this book.

ORGANIZATIONAL ASSESSMENT USING THE BALDRIGE MODEL

In 1987, the United States Congress instituted under public law the Malcolm Baldrige National Quality Award (Baldrige Award) as a national initiative to help industry and service organizations improve performance and become more efficient and competitive. The award is named after the late Malcolm Baldrige who died in a rodeo accident while serving as the Secretary of Commerce to the late President Ronald Reagan. The award criteria include an organizational assessment of performance in all dimensions: leadership; strategic planning and execution; customer focus; human resource management; process, product, and service management; information management; and customer, human resource, financial, and operational results. The process is gruelling, but worthwhile as organizations ask the tough questions that help establish performance excellence on all fronts.

The Baldrige Award was originally designed to encourage improvement in the quality of products and services from American companies. Over the past 15 years, the Baldrige criteria have emerged as a very effective holistic model for organizational assessments. The criteria are more an organization excellence model in that they enable organizations to carry out an assessment of their current performance relative to their stakeholder needs and put in place a set of processes and improvement plans resulting from the assessment to maximize stakeholder satisfaction. The criteria have generally been accepted on a global basis as a definition of performance excellence, with several other countries adopting either the exact set of criteria or minor variations of the same. For example, Europe created the European Foundation for Quality Management (EFQM) model, Australia developed the Australian National Quality Award, India uses the EFQM approach, and Japan modeled its Deming approach around the Baldrige criteria. Several major corporations such as HP (Hewlett Packard), Honeywell, IBM, Infosys, and the Tata companies in India are using (or have used) the Baldrige criteria for internal assessments. A number of state awards have sprung up all over the United States that further reinforce the claim of general acceptability of the model as the de facto definition of performance excellence.

The Baldrige criteria also serve as a catchall for several of the "other" quality initiatives such as ISO 9000, QS 9000, TL 9000, and Six Sigma that gained significance recently. Appendix B is an attempt to show the relationship between Baldrige and other quality assessment models.

Why would an Organization Use the Baldrige Criteria for Assessment?

There are several reasons why an organization would use the Baldrige criteria for self-assessment. The obvious one is that the assessment reveals significant areas that the organization can focus its efforts on to achieve performance excellence. The other reasons given by organizations that use the criteria for self-assessment include[1]:

- Customers and/or competitors are driving a need to change

- Your industry is changing

- Your organization is among the best, and you want to make sure you stay that way

- Business is good, and you want to keep it that way

- Your leadership team has committed to a self-assessment to enhance organizational learning

- Your organization's values are aligned with the core values of the Baldrige criteria

- You see a clear connection between your key issues and the systematic approach embodied in the Baldrige criteria for improving organizational performance practices

- You could capitalize on one or more of the following benefits of conducting a self-assessment and implementing action plans for improvement:

  ❑ jump-starting a change initiative

  ❑ energizing improvement initiatives

  ❑ focusing your organization on common goals

Numerous studies have been conducted to demonstrate the direct correlation between financial results and organizations that score well against the Baldrige criteria or otherwise have a strong, systematic approach to overall quality management.

The United States Department of Commerce, National Institute of Standards and Technology (NIST), that administers the Malcolm Baldrige National Quality Award developed a "Baldrige Index," a fictitious stock fund. The fund is made up of the publicly traded companies that have won the Baldrige Award since its inception in 1988. Results are published each year at its website (http://www.nist.gov) and are summarized in Figure 3.1. The "fund" looks at all the winners of the Baldrige award, but segments whole company winners from divisions or sub-section of larger companies. For instance, IBM Rochester is a division of the IBM Corporation and does not issue its own shares of stock. Also, a number of the business award winners are privately held, so they are excluded from the "fund." The stock price was tracked from the first day of the month after the award was announced. In 2002, the Baldrige Winners Index that included the whole company winners outperformed the S&P 500 by a ratio of nearly 4.5 to 1.[2] NIST also tracked the performance of all firms that won the award as a whole firm or as a division or subsidiary of a larger parent company. Thus,

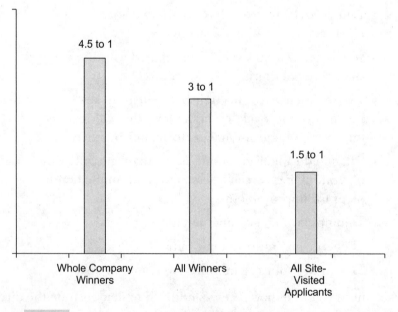

Fig. 3.1 NIST Baldrige Award Winners Stock Performance Index

the parent company performance of division winners was considered. This group of firms outperformed the S&P 500 by a ratio of 3 to 1. The publicly traded 1991–2000 site visited companies as a group (those organizations scored about 500 points out of 1000 to warrant a site visit), outperformed the S&P 500 by approximately 1.5 to 1.

Robinson Capital Management, an investment company in Minneapolis, Minnesota, has formed a real stock fund composed of companies that have a strong focus on quality and have demonstrated strong quality results. The results of this fund, shown in Figure 3.2, have significantly outperformed the S&P 500. Craig Robinson, president of Robinson Capital Management and the stock fund manager, says this is one of the strongest funds in the company's portfolio of funds.[3]

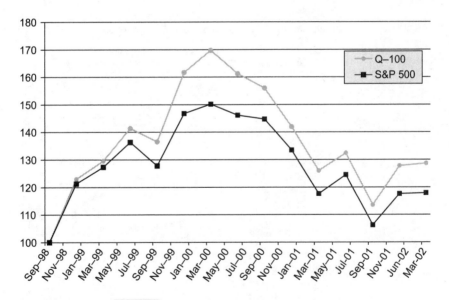

Fig. 3.2 Q-100 (General Securities, Inc.)

Another study, conducted by Dr. Vinod Singhall of Georgia Institute of Technology, examined the stock market performance of any quality award winner, not just Baldrige winners. The awards included industry awards, state awards, and the Baldrige Award, but all the awards were for quality performance.[4] About 600 award winners were identified, with about 75 percent coming from manufacturing industries. The stock performance was examined for a five-year period before winning the award and a five-year period after winning the award. To control industry differences, a control group was created. Each winner was paired with a firm from the same SIC classification and was the closest in size to the winner based on the book value of assets. There was no difference in performance measures or stock price in the five-year period before winning an award. However, that changed rather dramatically after an award was received. The award winners outperformed the control group by a ratio of 2 to 1 in the areas of operating income, sales, total assets, number of employees, return on sales and return on assets. The stock return for the award winners was 114 percent compared to 80 percent for the S&P 500. The award winners outperformed the S&P 500 by almost a 1.5 to 1 ratio. The results of this study are summarized in Figure 3.3.

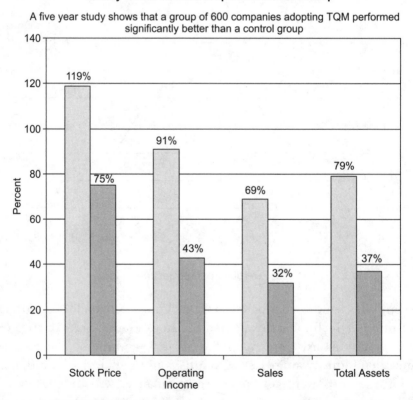

Fig. 3.3 Quality Award Winners Outperform Control Group

THE BALDRIGE CRITERIA

The Baldrige criteria have evolved over time and have become the de facto definition of performance excellence. The criteria embody 11 Core Values and are structured into seven categories. Each category is segmented into items and each item is segmented into several "Areas to Address." The areas to address are actual questions that beg an answer or a response to where the organization currently stands relative to that question. The key characteristics provided by the performance excellence model are:

- It is non prescriptive and needs to be adapted to the business

- Supports a system approach to maintaining an organizational-wide alignment facilitated by:

  — Results-oriented cause-effect linkages among criteria items

  — Connecting and reinforcing measures derived from the organization's strategy

  — Dynamic linkage through learning cycles such as planning, execution, assessment and revision

- Lends itself to a two-part diagnostic system that is built on 19 performance-oriented requirements (items) and three assessment dimensions (approach, deployment and results)

Figure 3.4 attempts to illustrate the elements of the three

Approach	Deployment	Results
• Appropriate	• Extent • Breadth	• Outcomes
• Effective	• Addressing Item Requirements	• Current Performance
• Systematic		• Relative Performance
• Integrated	• Appropriate Work Units	• Rate, Breadth, Importance of Performance
• Aligned		
• Fact Based		• Linkage to Measures
• Evaluation and Improvement Cycles		
• Innovative		
Category 1–6		Category 7

Fig. 3.4 The Performance Excellence Framework

assessment dimensions. Additional information on the Baldrige criteria can be found at http://www.nist.gov.[5]

In the following pages, the criteria for each category are explained, followed by a listing of key areas that the organization's senior management must address. Experience has shown that assimilating and responding to the criteria directly is an intricate task. However, if the sense in the criteria is distilled and translated into a set of questions or areas to address, the responses are more forthcoming. We need to remember to capture the responses in two dimensions—strengths and areas for improvements (or weaknesses). It should be noted that based on changes in the world economy and marketplace, the Baldrige criteria for performance excellence are dynamic and ever changing. Therefore, the criteria illustrated may or may not be current. It is recommended that the reader contact http://www.nist.gov for the latest set of criteria.[6]

Category 1: Leadership

1.1 Organizational Leadership

1.2 Public Responsibility and Citizenship

Impact on Society • Product, Services, Operations • Regulatory, Legal and Risks • Measures and Targets	**Public Concerns** • Current and Future Products, Services, Operations • Anticipate and Proactively Prepare

Ethical Business Practices
• All Stakeholder Transactions and Interactions

Support of Key Communities
• All Employees

Areas that Need to be Addressed by an Organization for Category 1

- A clearly defined, communicated, deployed, and reviewed mission, vision and values of the organization that are inspirational enough so as to be competitively superior.

- In setting directions for the organization, the senior leadership has a long-range view of the future and is based on customer/market needs, competitive information, including potential competition.

- The values are consistently reinforced and integrated with leadership selection, and employee behaviors are assessed as part of the performance appraisal process.

- An environment exists that promotes innovation and learning that allows organizations to remain at the cutting edge.

- Organizational reviews are a mix of financial and non-financial measures, are customer driven and cascaded across the organization to establish line of sight between corporate and individual goals.

- Mechanisms are in place to translate performance review findings into priorities for continuous and breakthrough improvement and they are deployed throughout the organization including suppliers and partners.

- A process is in place to promote organizational monitoring and performance evaluation of the board members including the CEO.

- Variety of approaches exist to improve leadership effectiveness that is more fact based and demonstrates evaluation and improvement cycles starting from the organization board down the chain.

- There is a clear delineation of key measures of corporate citizenship and public responsibility that are pertinent to the organization.

- Public concerns are anticipated well in advance and prevention based approaches are in place to address those issues.

Category 2: Strategic Planning

2.1 Strategy Development

Strategy Development Process
- Key steps and participants
- Customers and market needs/expectations
- Competitive environment and capabilities
- Financial, societal, and other potential risks
- Human resource capabilities and needs
- Operational capabilities and needs
- Supplier/partner capabilities and needs

Strategic Objectives
- Key strategic objectives and timetable
- Evaluating strategic options

Areas that Need to be Addressed by an Organization

- Existence of a robust planning process that has a strong focus on the strategies of the organization derived from the mission/vision.

- The planning process considers and uses various stakeholder data/information that helps the organization arrive at a set of strategic objectives capable of positioning the organization as the best of the best.

- Technology road maps have been assessed thoroughly and limitations thereof have been factored into the planning activity, including supply chain readiness.

- Evidence that financial, market and societal risks have been considered.

- Suppliers are positioned as partners to maximize supply chain efficiency and all related data is used as inputs to the planning process.

- Availability of data on all important processes, technologies, including information technology (IT) systems.

- Data on human resource (HR) potential, workforce attrition, and so forth.

- The set of strategic objectives is a good mix of financial and non-financial factors, the measures have long- and short-term goals with plans supporting the achievement of those goals.

2.2 Strategy Deployment

Areas that Need to be Addressed by an Organization

- Performance measures that map into the strategic objectives have been identified and have short- and long-term goals with associated action plans.

- Goals and targets cascade to all levels of the organization to establish complete alignment.

- HR plans are linked to the business plans, including staffing and allocation of resources.

- Close integration between the budgeting and the planning process.

- Projections of performance measures are realistic, tied to the vision of the organization and are competitively superior.

Category 3: Customer and Market Focus

3.1 Customer and Market Knowledge

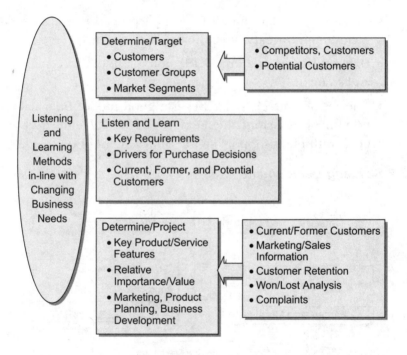

Areas that Need to be Addressed by the Organization

- Existence of a variety of listening and learning approaches to determine customer/market segments, product and service features specific to those segments.

- Use of comparative data on product/service features, complaints and gains/losses of customers to help determine customer requirements.

- A process is in place to analyze reasons for loss of customers.

- Identification of important trends in technology, competition, society, economy, demographics, etc., and how each of these will impact the business.

- Existence of a process to determine future customer requirements, use of such data in designing new or enhanced products and services that will enable the organization to be "ahead of the curve" when positioning new products in the market place.

3.2 a. Customer Relationships

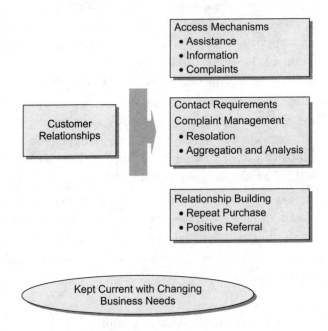

3.2 b. Customer Satisfaction Determination

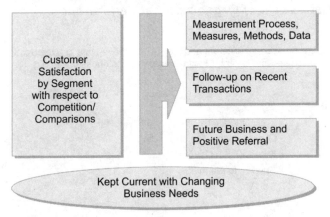

Areas that Need to be Addressed by the Organization

- Efficiency of access mechanisms that enable customers to comment, complain or seek assistance.

- Definition of key customer contact points and most important requirements for each transaction.

- Comprehensive complaint management process, existence of a process for analyzing root causes of the complaints, generating trends, transferring the knowledge gained to other divisions of the organization, as appropriate, and verification with the customer upon closing the complaint.

- Multiple approaches to determine customer satisfaction, again existence of a process for analyzing root causes of areas of dissatisfaction, transferring the knowledge gained to other divisions of the organization, as appropriate, and verification with the customer upon resolving the issue.

- Existence of service standards for all customer contact personnel, deployment of these across the organization and performance to these standards tracked as part of the appraisal process.

- Existence of a variety of approaches/methods to build customer loyalty.

Category 4: Measurement, Analysis and Knowledge Management

4.1 Measurement of Organizational Performance

1. Measures/Indicators and Key Comparative Data and Information Selection, Extent, Effectiveness, Completeness, Reliability
2. Data Analysis

- Daily Operations
- Organizational Performance
- Improvement Options
- Support to Planning

Kept Current with Changing Business Needs

Areas that Need to be Addressed by the Organization

- Existence of a sound performance measurement system that has a good balance of financial and non-financial measures.
- The chosen measures have a good tie-in with the strategic objectives or the key business drivers derived in Category 2.0.
- Comparative data is available for all the measures.
- Analysis of data/information is consistent with the initiatives undertaken in the organization.
- Existence of a process to correlate improvements in product and service quality measures to improvements in customer satisfaction levels.
- Evidence that major business decisions are based on analysis of data and an understanding of how each measure relates to others.

4.2 Information and Knowledge Management

Data and Information Availability	Organizational Knowledge

Data Accessibility
  • Employees
  • Customers
  • Suppliers/Partners
	• Knowledge Sharing across the Organization
	• Transfer of Relevant Knowledge from Customers, Suppliers and Partners

	Reliability of Hardware/Software Systems
Data Integrity/Reliability	• User Friendly

Areas that Need to be Addressed by the Organization

- Data and information are accessible to all stakeholders including customers, suppliers and partners as appropriate.
- Data integrity and reliability are constantly evaluated.
- Evidence of a process to determine the satisfaction levels of the users of the systems in the organization and corrective actions thereof.

- Process to identify and share best practices, transfer knowledge across the organization including those from customers, suppliers and partners, as appropriate.

Category 5: Human Resource Focus

5.1 Work Systems

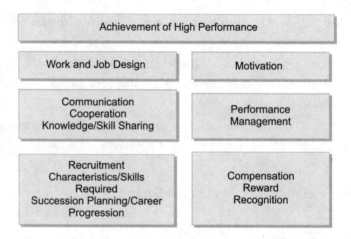

Areas that Need to be Addressed by the Organization

- Design and organization of work and jobs to promote high flexibility, multi-skilling, job rotations, etc., that ultimately enhance teamwork.

- Human Resource (HR) plans relative to employee development, work and job designs, compensation and job benefits, recruitment and selection. They should be tied to the business plans in Category 2.0 and the organization must have clearly identified short- and long-term goals for each of the HR elements.

- Consistent implementation of performance management systems across different levels and units in the organization.

- Performance management systems to reinforce customer and business focus.

- Existence of a process for effective succession planning for senior leadership, and at other levels in the organization, that facilitates smooth transition in the event of positions falling vacant.

- Methods and approaches are in place to recognize organizational skill set needs and the hiring policy is consistent with those methods. A process exists to evaluate the skill sets and keep in-line with the business needs as the latter changes.

5.2 Employee Learning and Motivation

Areas that Need to be Addressed by the Organization

- Existence of a process for identification of training needs, assessment of current skill set gaps in relation to the business plans (Category 2) and fixing those gaps.

- Methods exist to obtain input from across the workforce and use them to determine training needs.

- Methods to deliver education and training are based on inputs obtained from employees.

- Existence of a process to evaluate the effectiveness of training, e.g., ROI on dollars spent on training.

- Customer contact employees possess all the relevant skills appropriate to that function and performance measures are in place and tied to the employee performance appraisal process (Item 3.2 a).

5.3 Employee Well-Being and Satisfaction

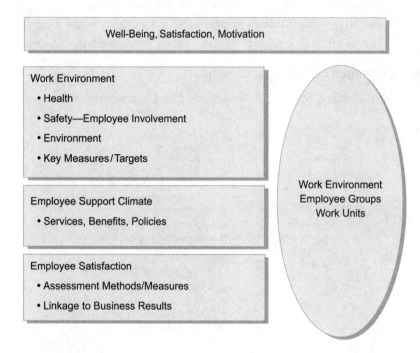

Well-Being, Satisfaction, Motivation

Work Environment
- Health
- Safety—Employee Involvement
- Environment
- Key Measures/Targets

Employee Support Climate
- Services, Benefits, Policies

Employee Satisfaction
- Assessment Methods/Measures
- Linkage to Business Results

Work Environment
Employee Groups
Work Units

Areas that Need to be Addressed by the Organization

- A systematic process is in place to enable the organization to understand the needs of its employees (all categories and types of employees; all locations; all parts of the organization).

- Focus is on the current dissatisfiers and the action plans drive those dissatisfiers to a satisfactory resolution that could be determined either in the performance appraisal process or in the employee satisfaction surveys.

- Employee satisfaction surveys capture current trends in addressing dissatisfiers specific and relevant to different employee groups and cover different levels in the organization.

- Programs for employee assistance.

- Methods in place to correlate improvements in employee satisfaction to business results.

Category 6: Process Management

6.1 Value Creation Processes

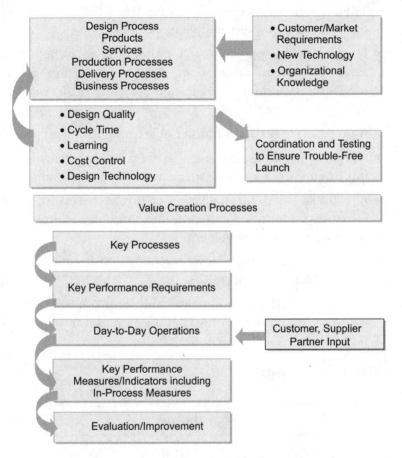

Areas that Need to be Addressed by the Organization

- Existence of a process for translating customer requirements into product and service designs that cover the full life cycle.

- Provision of a prevention-based approach that is built into the design process, for example, reviews at the different stages of the life cycle.

- Involvement of appropriate interfaces across the organization during reviews so that the right inputs are factored into the design process to enable a trouble-free product or service launch.

- The organization has identified all business processes (non-product specific/non-service specific) and their associated measures.

- These business processes have been derived after synthesizing inputs from customers, suppliers/partners.

- Key performance measures/indicators are identified for all value creation processes (e.g., design, production/delivery, service and business) and communicated to all, including suppliers/partners.

- A process is in place for transfer of learning from past projects.

- All value creating processes are constantly evaluated for improvements in appropriate measures (e.g., cycle time).

- A process exists for tracking performance relative to the measures identified, including ongoing supply base monitoring and management.

- A constant effort to improve supplier performance and the supplier management process.

- A constant effort to evaluate and improve the business processes in place, ensuring that they are in line with current business needs and directions.

6.2 Support Processes

Support processes
• Key Processes and Requirements–Inputs from Customers (Internal and External), Suppliers, and Partners • Design • Performance Monitoring • Key Performance Measures/Indicators • Minimize Cost of Inspection • Evaluation and Improvement

Areas that Need to be Addressed by the Organization

- The organization has identified all support processes and their associated measures.

- A process exists to ensure all the support process requirements have been derived based on the needs of the customer(s) requirements (external/internal), and includes suppliers and partners as appropriate.
- Support processes are aligned with the value creation processes.
- Key performance indicators have been identified, tracked and monitored to ultimately enhance internal customer satisfaction.
- An approach exists to evaluate and improve the performance of support processes.

Category 7: Business Results

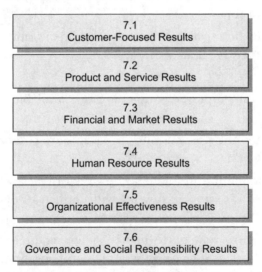

Areas that Need to be Addressed by the Organization

7.1

- Results are available, by market or customer group, on customer satisfaction.
- Trends show continual improvements over the last several years in all measures of customer satisfaction.
- Results are compared to competition for all customer satisfaction attributes/requirements as discussed in Item 3.1.

- Results/data on customer loyalty and value perception are clearly superior to industry averages and major competition.
- Results/data are available on losses of customers and that they show decreasing trends.

7.2

- Results are available for all products and services and mirror well with the measures identified in Item 6.1 and data in Item 4.1.
- Trends indicate sustained improvements over a period of time, are ahead of competition and comparable to industry benchmarks.

7.3

- Results demonstrate marketshare performance is ahead of competition and that the performance is sustained over a period of time.
- Similarly, financial results show the organization is competitively superior on all attributes.

7.4

- Results on employee satisfaction are available by employee group.
- Data on employee assistance programs are comparable to the industry best.
- Education and training data show the organization is a leader in providing its employees with effective developmental opportunities.
- Results show that performance system changes to the work systems such as suggestion systems, compensation, recognition and other approaches lead to improvements in financial performance.
- Similarly, a strong correlation exists between an increase in employee satisfaction and business results or the strategic objectives in Item 2.2.

7.5

- Results are available for all the in-process measures identified in Items 6.1, 6.2, and, as before, demonstrate superior performance relative to industry best.

7.6

- Audit results (internal and external) show no adverse trends and no incidents/concerns have ever been found.

- Data on environmental performance and other measures of public responsibility have a tie in with Item 1.2.

- Levels and trends in regulatory compliance results have no adverse findings.

SOME USEFUL HINTS REGARDING ORGANIZATIONAL ASSESSMENTS

In the opinion of the authors, in the methodology suggested above, the criteria and the impact come across more powerfully if the sequence shown in Figure 3.5 is followed. In other words, instead of going over the criteria in a sequential order, one can work on a reordered sequence that facilitates better engagement and connection with the senior management.

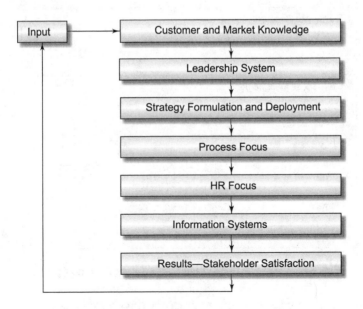

Fig. 3.5 Suggested Assessment Sequence

It would also be useful to remember that the Baldrige criteria need to be viewed in a holistic sense so as to maximize the power of the

Baldrige model. In other words, one needs to recognize the linkages among and between the various criteria elements shown in Figure 3.6. Whatever method is used for organizational diagnostics, to present an integrated picture, the linkages need to be noted and applied appropriately.

Item	Linkage
1.0 Leadership	
1.1	2.1, 2.2, 3.1, 4.1, 5.1, 5.2, 6.1, 6.2
1.2	2.2, 7.5
2.0 Strategic Planning	
2.1	1.1, 3.1, 4.1, 5.1, 6.3
2.2	1.1, 3.1, 4.1, 5.1, 5.2, 5.3, 6.1, 6.2, 7.1-6
3.0 Customer and Market Focus	
3.1	3.2, 6.1
3.2	2.2, 3.1, 4.1, 7.1
4.0 Measurement, Analysis, and Knowledge Management	
4.1	2.1, 2.2, 4.1, 6.1-2, 7.1-6
4.2	2.1, 4.1, 5.1
5.0 Human Resource Focus	
5.1	1.1, 2.2, 7.3
5.2	1.1, 3.2, 5.1, 6.1-2, 7.3
5.3	2.2, 4.1, 7.3
6.0 Process Management	
6.1	2.1, 2.2, 3.1, 4.1, 4.2, 7.5
6.2	2.1, 2.2, 3.1, 4.1, 5.2, 7.5
7.0 Business Results	
7.1	2.2, 3.1, 3.2, 4.1
7.2	2.2, 3.1, 3.2, 4.1, 6.1
7.3	2.2, 4.1, 6.1
7.4	2.2, 4.1, 5.1, 5.2, 5.3
7.5	2.2, 4.1, 6.1, 6.2
7.6	1.1, 1.2, 2.2, 5.1

Fig. 3.6 Linkages of Baldrige Criteria Items to One Another

USING THE APPLICATION APPROACH TO ASSESS AN ORGANIZATION

When we want to carry out an assessment using the application approach, the underlying principles are the same. However, in this case, perhaps, one has the advantage of an independent evaluation that provides a more objective assessment.

In the application approach, responses to the criteria requirements need to be documented in a 50-page application that can then be submitted to any state quality award or to the Baldrige process. Most state awards follow the Baldrige process in that the application is evaluated by a set of trained examiners and the report is captured in a document that identifies strengths and opportunities for improvement for each of the 19 items of the criteria and, in addition, provide a score on a 1 to 1000 scale. This helps the organization to calibrate their position and also get an idea of what needs to be done to bridge the gap. As stated earlier, the biggest benefit of this approach is the independent evaluation with a list of key organizational strengths and opportunities.

Figure 3.7 gives a high-level view of the relation between the scores of an organization at different levels of maturity and what that means to the organization in relationship to their improvement activities. The National Institute of Science and Technology (NIST) website provides examples of organizational assessments of different types of organizations (large company, small business, health care, education) that can be used as a model before beginning (http://www.nist.gov).[7] Most of these organizations score in the range of 400 to 500 points.

ALTERNATIVE ASSESSMENT APPROACHES

Over the years, organizations have employed several approaches to assessments using the Baldrige criteria. Some of the more common ones are[8, 9]:

- Workshop/interview assessments
- Surveys
- Senior management assessments
- Mock application
- Audits

In the opinion of the authors a combination of some of the above approaches needs to be put in place keeping in mind the level of executive commitment and the organization's acceptance of this

Score	Interpretation
1–250	Beginnings of a systematic approach to the basic purposes of the criteria; major gaps exist in deployment; results not reported for many to most areas of importance to the organization's key performance requirements.
250–400	An effective systematic approach responsive to the basic purposes of the criteria; deployment is in the initial stages; results reported for many to most areas of importance to the organization's key performance requirements.
400–600	Systematic approach, responsive to the overall purpose of the criteria, well-deployed and a fact-based evaluation and improvement process is in place; some trends evaluated against relevant comparisons/benchmarks.
600–800	Systematic approach, responsive to the multiple requirements of the criteria, well-deployed with no gaps; fact-based evaluation and improvement process supported by clear evidence of refinement and improved integration as a result of organizational level analysis and learning; results compare favorably with relevant comparisons and benchmarks and address most key customer, market and process requirements.
800–100	Systematic approach fully responsive to all the requirements of the criteria; fully deployed; strong refinement and integration backed by excellent organizational level analysis and learning; evidence of industry and benchmark leadership demonstrated in many areas.

Fig. 3.7 Scoring Matrix

paradigm. For example, surveys may well be a method to kick-start a program where a sample of the employees respond to the survey questions and the responses are analyzed to get a first-cut view of the organization's status on the current situation. Some of the findings could then be validated using a more formal approach—the senior management's assessment. In this method, the senior management in an organization—the CEO and those who report to him or her directly—are asked to participate in a two-day off-site (preferably) meeting facilitated by someone who is very familiar with the Baldrige criteria. The findings are captured in a two-dimensional format which typically covers the strengths and areas for improvement specific to the organization. A sample is shown in Figure 3.8. One can then drive more precision into the findings by working on a mock application or, better still, submitting a 50-page application to the state or to the Baldrige process. The latter provides an independent evaluation, regarded as the biggest gain of that exercise, notwithstanding the effort required to turn in that application.

Strengths	Opportunities for improvement
• Senior leaders of the organization communicate and reinforce short- and long-term direction, performance expectations, and organizational values through quarterly meetings with employees, monthly messages passed down the management chain, handbooks that clarify senior management's expectations, and articles in the organization's daily newsletters.	• Although senior leaders in the organization have created an environment for employee learning, it is not clear how senior leaders empower employees, encourage innovation, and promote organizational and individual learning.
• Senior leaders and employees of the organization actively support the organization's key communities through direct involvement in civic organizations and charitable contributions.	• It is not clear how senior leaders are using organizational performance review findings to improve the leadership system and their own effectiveness. This makes it difficult to establish whether the leadership system has undergone any changes in response to changing market conditions and if it is in line with business needs.

Fig. 3.8   Sample of List of Strengths and Areas for Improvement

Workshop/Interview Assessment

The workshop/interview approach, conducted with the senior leaders of the organization, typically at an off-site location over two days, has been used very effectively by several organizations. At such sessions, each category is explained and responses are sought relative to the strengths and weaknesses of the organization. This is done by focusing on the key areas to be addressed with regard to the Baldrige criteria requirements. If the assessment is carried out in a workshop mode, then it may be useful to divide the participants into four or five groups of four or five people. One can cover three categories on the first day and the remaining categories on the second day. At the end of the two-day session, the facilitator can aggregate all the findings into one consolidated report.

Surveys

To help organizations conduct simple assessments using the Baldrige criteria as a base, several versions of an online assessment tool have been developed. An online survey is sent to all types of employees in all areas of the organization. The numerical results and comments from the survey are used to create a generic set of organizational strengths and weaknesses. Narrative responses are allowed and recorded. The listing of these comments provides some additional insight into specific strengths and opportunities that can constitute focused improvement efforts. Several organizations have successfully used this method as an entry tool to assess organizational performance in the early stages. A number of state award programs offer this tool as an alternative to writing a 50-page application. Additional information can be obtained at the Wisconsin Forward Award office.[10]

Senior Management Assessments

Senior managers may attempt to do a quick assessment of the organization by using information already gathered or known. In this approach, the senior management typically employs the use of an independent, unbiased consultant, either from within or outside the organization, to identify the key strengths and weaknesses of the organization as a whole. This approach is sometimes used as a preamble at the start of the strategic planning process, and information about the organization is limited primarily to input by the senior management.

Mock Application

An organization may choose to assess itself fully against the Baldrige model and write an internal application that addresses all the criteria, with or without regard to content (other than accuracy) and page count. This method allows the organization to document and record approaches and processes that address the criteria, and to assess its relative strengths and opportunities based on these findings. Significant gaps are readily apparent as little or no evidence may exist for a particular Item. In this approach, an organization may employ examiners, either internal or external to the organization, who understand the criteria and the scoring process. The mock application may be used as a preamble to writing a full 50-page application as part of a state or national award process.

Audit Approach

In contrast to the other four approaches, this approach is perhaps more objective and expensive. The approach is similar to the workshop/interview approach, except that there is no written application and the assessments are carried out through interviews, review of data, and observations. Numerous interviews are carried out throughout the organization to gather the information and evidence in support of the criteria, or to determine the lack of evidence thereof.

USING ASSESSSMENT FINDINGS FOR ORGANIZATIONAL IMPROVEMENT

If done correctly, assessing an organization against the Baldrige criteria will provide a list of key strengths and areas for improvement. The organization needs to capitalize on its strengths and use them to differentiate itself from its competitors. The organization should look at means to pervasively address the opportunities for improvement. It should take a "systems" approach to defining ways to address the issues. In other words, the areas for improvement probably reflect pervasive issues across more than one part of the organization. Therefore, the fix needs to be broad in nature and scope. Most organizations use the results of their assessments against the Baldrige criteria as input for their strategic planning processes. Because of the pervasive use of the Baldrige criteria for organization improvement, there are numerous organizations that have conducted assessments of themselves and are willing to share key learnings. The annual "Quest for Excellence" conducted by the Baldrige National Quality Program, National Institute of Standards and Technology, US Department of Commerce, highlights present and past Baldrige winners along with best practices.[11] The organizations present at this event are eager to share what they have learned along their quality journey, including significant vulnerabilities and major obstacles they have overcome.

At this point, it would be useful to not only prioritize and generate a time-bound action plan by consolidating the areas for improvement (weaknesses), it may be a better idea to identify the "big hitters" the organization needs to focus on to impact customers. We could refer to this listing as the processes that need the organization's immediate attention (we will elaborate on this topic in Chapter 7). In any case, a lot of effort has gone into determining the key opportunities for the organization and it is up to the management to use this information in an effective and constructive manner for organizational improvement.

SUMMARY

The Performance for Excellence criteria embodied by the Malcolm Baldrige National Quality Award provide one of the most comprehensive and robust models that can be used to assess an organization's performance. There is undisputed research that demonstrates a direct correlation between scores and findings from Baldrige assessments, and overall organization performance, including key factors such as profitability, stock price, and revenues. The criteria have evolved over the last 15 years and are used as the basis for state and international quality assessment programs. Although the criteria are sometimes considered synonymous with quality awards, they are more about organization performance and excellence, and use of the criteria through different methods does not position this model as a means for winning awards. The assessment results in findings that the organization can use to make strategic improvements. The findings can be translated into a scoring band that the organization can use to determine improvement from assessment to assessment, or to compare itself to others.

It is the authors' opinion, based upon years of experience working with different assessment models and types of organizations, that the Baldrige criteria provide the best model for assessing strengths and opportunities for improvements that impact an organization's ability to invoke improvement and effective change.

REFERENCES

(1) "Getting Started with the Baldrige National Quality Program," April 2001, NIST0055, Baldrige National Quality Program, National Institute of Standards and Technology, Administration Building, Room A600, 100 Bureau Drive, Stop 1020, Gaithersburg, Maryland 20899-1020, USA. http://www.nist.gov/

(2) "Why Apply?," 2001, NIST0054, Baldrige National Quality Program, National Institute of Standards and Technology, Administration Building, Room A600, 100 Bureau Drive, Stop 1020, Gaithersburg, Maryland 20899-1020, USA. http://www.nist.gov/

(3) Published in the proceedings from the 49th Minnesota Quality Conference, Radisson Hotel South, Bloomington, Minnesota, USA, July 22–24, 2002, "Customer-Centered Six Sigma" keynote presentation by Steven H. Hoisington.

(4) "Customer Centered Six Sigma: Linking Customers, Process Improvement, and Financial Results," ASQ Quality Press, Milwaukee, Wisconsin, USA, 2001, by Earl Naumann and Steven H. Hoisington.

(5) United States Department of Commerce, Technology Administration, National Institute of Standards and Technology, Baldrige National Quality Award Program, Administration Building, Room A635, 100 Bureau Drive, Stop 1020, Gaithersburg, Maryland 20899-1020, USA. http://www.nist.gov/

(6) Ibid.

(7) Ibid.

(8) "Baldrige Award Winning Quality"—Tenth edition—How to interpret the Baldrige criteria for performance excellence: Mark Graham Brown-ASQ, ASQ Quality Press, Milwaukee, Wisconsin, USA.

(9) "Insights to Performance Excellence 2003: An Inside Look at the 2003 Baldrige Award Criteria," ASQ Quality Press, Milwaukee, Wisconsin, USA, 2003, by Mark L. Blazey.

(10) Elizabeth C. Menzer, Executive Director, Wisconsin Forward Award, Inc., 2909 Landmark Place, Suite 110, Madison, Wisconsin 53703, USA, (608) 663-5300, http://www.forwardaward.org/

(11) "Quest for Excellence", United States Department of Commerce, Technology Administration, National Institute of Standards and Technology, Baldrige National Quality Award Program, Administration Building, Room A635, 100 Bureau Drive, Stop 1020, Gaithersburg, Maryland 20899-1020, USA. http://www.nist.gov/

ASSESSING ORGANIZATIONAL CAPABILITIES— EFQM AND SEI/CMM

The authors are firm believers in the value of the Baldrige model to assess an organization's capabilities. As illustrated in Chapter 3, a solid financial and operational performance is attributable to those organizations that embrace the Baldrige criteria and score well on its assessments. There are other widely accepted organizational assessment models besides the Baldrige criteria and the authors would be remiss not to include a discussion of some of these models in this book. The authors are also experienced and well-versed in the use of numerous assessment models and have used them in one capacity or another. The other two noteworthy models are the European Foundation for Quality Management (EFQM)[1] and the SEI [Software] Capability Maturity Model (SEI/CMM)[2] used primarily for companies that develop software.

EFQM CRITERIA FOR BUSINESS EXCELLENCE

The European Foundation for Quality Management (EFQM) is a membership-based not-for-profit organization, founded in 1988 by 14 leading European businesses, with a mission to be the driving force for sustainable business excellence in Europe and a vision of a world in which European organizations excel.

To help promote sustainable excellence in European organizations, the EFQM has promoted partnership with similar national organizations in Europe. All of these organizations have worked with the EFQM to develop the fundamental concepts of excellence and to promote the EFQM excellence model.

The model shown in Figure 4.1 is very similar in form and structure to the Baldrige model discussed in Chapter 3. It has nine categories to address and is based on the premise that:

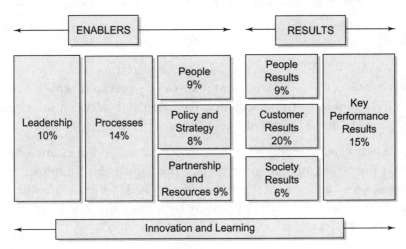

Fig. 4.1 The EFQM Model

"Excellent results with respect to Performance, Customers, People, and Society are achieved through Leadership driving Policy and Strategy, which are delivered through People, Partnerships and Resources, and Processes."

The arrows emphasize the dynamic nature of the model. They show that innovation and learning help to improve enablers, which in turn lead to improved results.

Figure 4.1 identifies the terms "enablers" and "results" that are used to designate two categories of the criteria. Enabler criteria are concerned with how the organization undertakes key activities; results criteria are concerned with the results that are being achieved.

At the heart of the model lies the RADAR logic. The elements of RADAR are results, approach, deployment, assessment, and review. The last four are used in the enabler criteria and the results element is used in the results criteria.

This logic states that an organization needs to:

- Determine the results it is aiming for. This has to be a part of its policy and strategy making process. These results cover the performance of the organization, both financially and operationally, and the perceptions of its stakeholders.

- Plan and develop an integrated set of sound approaches to deliver the required results both now and in the future.

- Deploy the approaches in a systematic way to ensure full implementation.

- Assess and review the approaches that are being followed based on monitoring and analysis of the results achieved and ongoing learning activities. Based on this, identify, prioritize, plan and implement improvements needed.

When using the model within an organization, for example, for the purposes of self-assessment, the approach, deployment, assessment, and review elements of the RADAR logic should be addressed for each enabler sub-criterion and the results element should be addressed for each results sub-criterion.

Applying RADAR Logic

The specific elements of the RADAR concept are described below.

Results

Results cover the achievements of an organization. In an excellent organization, the results will show positive trends and/or sustained good performance, targets will be appropriate and met or exceeded, performance will compare well with others and will be a result of approaches adopted. Additionally, the scope of the results will address the relevant areas.

Approach

Approach covers an organization's plans and the reasons behind such plans. In an excellent organization, the approach will be sound—a clear rationale with well-defined and developed processes, and a clear focus on stakeholder needs. It will be integrated, supporting policy and strategy, and linked to other approaches where appropriate.

Deployment

Deployment covers the extent to which an organization uses the approach and what it does to deploy it. In an excellent organization, the approach will be implemented in relevant areas in a systematic way.

Assessment and Review

This covers an organization's assessment and review of the approach and its deployment. In an excellent organization, the approach and its deployment will be subject to regular measurement, learning activities will be undertaken, and the output from both will be used to identify, prioritize, plan, and implement improvement.

Organizational Assessment using EFQM Model

All the methods/approaches cited in Chapter 3 for organizational assessments using the Baldrige criteria are amenable to assessments using the EFQM criteria.

While the assessments typically result in identification of Strengths and Areas for Improvement, very much like how these had been identified in Chapter 3 using the Baldrige assessment model, some important differences need to be noted, especially when it is necessary to score a written application for an organization. These differences are illustrated in Figure 4.2.

The SEI/CMM model applies primarily to those organizations that develop software. However, due to the robust nature of the model, it can be applied to organizations of any type with very favorable results.

Baldrige[3]	EFQM[4]
1. There are a total of seven categories to address	1. There are a total of nine categories to address
2. The 'Results' (Category 7) section carries 450 points and the rest of the categories 550 points	2. The 'Results' and 'Enablers' sections each carry 500 points
3. The scoring is done at the item level	3. When a category is scored, each of the subtending areas to address carry equal weightage and need to be scored individually and finally rolled up to the category level
4. There are no weightages allocated either at the item level or at the category level	4. The categories themselves carry weightages (see Figure 4.1). For example, Category 1 carries 10%. Hence the category score obtained in Step 3 will then need to be multiplied by 10% and so on for the remainder of the categories Summation of individual category scores then results in the final score of the organization on a scale of 1–1000 For the Results section: • 6a takes 75% and 6b takes 25% of the points allocated to Category 6 • Similarly, 7a takes 75% and 7b 25% for Category 7 and the same holds good for Categories 8 and 9
5. The underlying focus with Baldrige is centered on customer and market needs	5. The underlying focus with EFQM is on five process(es)
6. The number of pages is limited to 50 when submitting a Baldrige application	6. The number of pages is limited to 75 when submitting an EFQM application

Fig. 4.2 Comparison between Baldrige and EFQM

SEI/CMM MODEL

As a major consumer of software products, the US Government recognized that the software industry was, and in many cases still is, in its infancy, when it began experiencing some of the resultant problems (e.g., receiving custom-developed products that were late, did not work, and were over budget). Therefore, in the 1980s, it chartered an organization to study existing problems and characterize sound practices that would help alleviate the problems. Thus, the Software Engineering Institute (SEI) was born. Associated with the Carnegie Mellon University, it provides leadership in advancing the practice of software engineering. The SEI came up with a model for software called the Capability Maturity Model (CMM) to cover key areas that needed attention in the development of a software product. It lays out these key areas and associates them with levels of maturity for a software organization.

In November 1986, the SEI, with assistance from the MITRE Corporation, began developing a model that would address the process maturity of an organization involved in the development and delivery of software. This model was based on two methods—software process assessment and software capability evaluation—as well as a maturity questionnaire. The CMM model is based on actual practices. However, it attempts to focus attention on the best practices.

Customer Focus and CMM

The CMM provides an evolutionary path to allow an organization to increase its software process maturity in stages. The ultimate goal is focused on meeting customer needs, both in the present and the future. The CMM is an application of performance improvement and process management to the software development industry. They should be aligned with the business needs of an organization and with other improvement activities undertaken within the organization.

The CMM is strongly focused on customer satisfaction as a goal. The driver behind the formation of the SEI, and the CMM itself, was that the end customer, the Department of Defense, was unhappy with its software contractors. The model provides excellent guidance to the strengths, weaknesses, and risks of selecting a specific software vendor, and to monitor a software contract.

While the model does not explicitly address the issue of customer delight, it describes how the customer and supplier should work in unison to ensure that customer requirements are well understood.

Structure of the SEI CMM

The SEI CMM advocates continuous process improvement. This approach is based on small evolutionary steps to be taken by an organization to gradually improve in process maturity. The CMM provides a framework that organizes these improvement steps into five maturity levels. Each level lays the foundation for the successive level of improvement. This approach helps an organization to prioritize its improvement efforts and work toward achievable goals. The CMM defines a continuous model. An organization is considered at Level 1 until assessed and found to be at a higher level. It must advance in stages to the subsequent levels. In other words, an organization cannot be assessed at Level 3 before first having been assessed at Level 1 and then at Level 2. Each level builds on the other. An organization will find it counterproductive to skip a level. With the exception of Level 1, each maturity level of the CMM addresses key process areas (KPA) as shown in Figure 4.3. These are the areas that an organization should focus on to improve its processes.

Each key process area identifies a related set of activities that, when performed collectively, achieve a set of goals that are considered important milestones to achieving process maturity and thus enhancing an organization's capability. To achieve the goals, the model advocates that the organization have policies in place. In addition, the model defines certain common features or attributes that help measure the effectiveness of the implementation and institutionalization of a key process area. It helps an organization determine if a process is implemented such that it is effective, repeatable, and lasting. These common features must be in place at every level of process maturity. The five common features are:

- Commitment to perform
- Ability to perform
- Activities performed

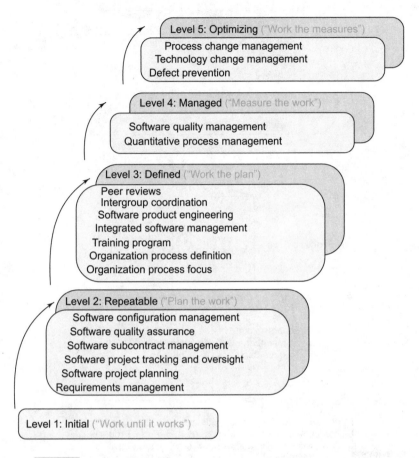

Fig. 4.3 SEI Capability Maturity Model for Software Development

- Measurement and analysis
- Verifying implementation

Figure 4.4 provides an overview of the structure of the CMM, and how a key process area is structured. The figure depicts the requirements management key process area at Level 2 of the model. It shows that by adequately performing the activities of the key process area, the goals of the key process area will be satisfied. For the activities to be successfully performed, the institutionalized common features must be in place. Figure 4.4 illustrates the alignment of activities and goals to the key process area.

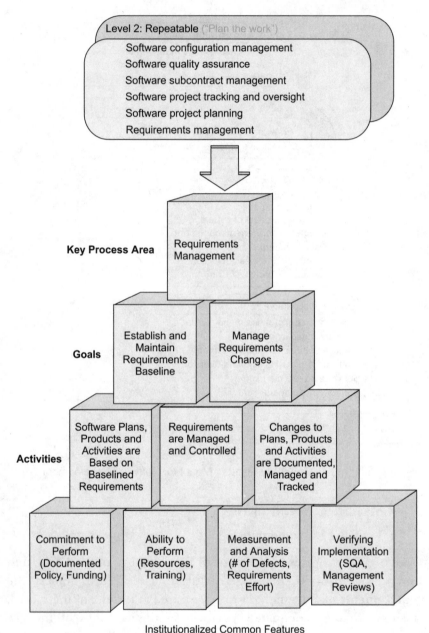

Fig. 4.4   Structure of the CMM

The alignment of key practices to goals is shown in Figure 4.5 that, for the requirements management key process area, illustrates the activities that must be performed to meet the goal and the

Goals	Requires that	Common Features
Goal 1: System requirements allocated to software are controlled to establish a baseline for software engineering and management. *Goal 2:* Software plans, products, and activities are kept consistent with the system requirements allocated to software.	*Activity 1:* The software engineering group reviews the allocated requirements before they are incorporated into the software project. *Activity 2:* The software engineering group uses the allocated requirements as the basis for software plans, work products, and activities. *Activity 3:* Changes to the allocated requirements are reviewed and incorporated into the software project.	*Commitment 1:* The project follows a written organizational policy for managing the system requirements allocated to software. *Ability 1:* For each project, responsibility is established for analyzing the system requirements and allocating them to hardware, software, and other system requirements *Ability 2:* The allocated requirements are documented. *Ability 3:* Adequate resources and funding are provided for managing the allocated requirements. *Ability 4:* Members of the software engineering group and other software related groups are trained to perform their requirements management activities. *Measurement 1:* Measurements are made and used to determine the status of the activities for managing the allocated requirements. *Verification 1:* The activities to manage the allocated require-ments are reviewed with senior management on a periodic basis. *Verification 2:* The activities to manage the allocated requirements are reviewed with the project manager on both a periodic and event-driven basis. *Verification 3:* The Software Quality Assurance group reviews and/or audits the activities and work products to manage the allocated require-ments and reports the results.

Fig. 4.5 Map of Goals, Requirements, and Features

applicable common features that must be implemented to ensure successful completion of the activities. These common features determine the ability of the organization to perform the activities, and provide policy as well as oversight through measurement and verification.

Finally, Figure 4.6 illustrates how an organization can determine whether it has satisfied the intent of the requirements management key process area. The information is presented in a chart depicting criteria for entry, task, verification, and exit. This step results in the identification of any deficiencies the organization needs to address and correct before proceeding to the next level. This step will identify required resources as well as deficient process steps or procedures.

ENTRY	TASK	EXIT
Policy (Co1)	Requirements reviewed (Ac1)	Requirements allocated to software baselined (Go1)
Responsibility (Ab1)	Requirements used as basis for further work (Ac2)	Software plans, products, activities kept consistent with allocated requirements (Go2)
Resources (Ab3)	Changes reviewed and incorporated (Ac3)	Records of reviews
Training (Ab4)		
	VERIFICATION	
	Senior management reviews (Ve1)	
	Project management review (Ve2)	
	SQA review/audit (Ve3)	

Fig. 4.6 Entry, Task, Verification, Exit (ETVX) Matrix

Successful Implementation of the CMM

As with the other assessment models described in this book, management involvement and commitment is required if the CMM is to succeed. The top management of the organization must actively decide on goals and a realistic implementation schedule. They must demonstrate a "commitment to perform" by providing the resources, communicating to the organization, and staying involved by monitoring the progress of the project.

It is suggested that a core team of motivated individuals be selected to conduct the organizational assessment using the CMM. The members should understand software development and effective auditing techniques. At least one team member, preferably someone from outside the organization, should serve as the team lead and be certified to conduct a CMM assessment. Once the core team has been selected, the top management, with assistance from the core team, must scope out the areas of the organization in which the CMM-based improvement will be implemented.

Following this, the core team must undergo training in the CMM methodology and in performing a CMM-based assessment. The newly trained assessors must then carry out a series of gap analyses in the various areas identified. The gap analyses will concentrate on the key process areas of CMM Level 2. Findings of the gap analyses must be captured and action or issues registered, with trends identified. In addition, any software related metrics that are collected and analyzed must be assessed.

At this point, the organization will have a fair assessment of its strengths and weaknesses. The top management must be apprised of the findings. The organization is now ready to take the next steps.

Initiating a CMM-Based Improvement Program

Once the assessment findings start getting recorded, the organization needs to begin the improvement process. Several key decisions will have to be made. These decisions will determine the outcome and success not only of the CMM-based improvement program, but also of the organization.

Decisions that must be made at this time are dependent on the nature of the organization's businesses. They include determining the following key items:

- What constitutes an organization
- At what level of the organization will measurements be analyzed for continuous improvement programs

If the organization has vastly differing business lines, it may want to designate that each business line constitutes an organization. Many organizations may be tempted to determine that country or site-specific locations are designated to constitute their own organizations. This is a natural outcome for organizations that have followed an improvement model based on the ISO 9000 standard. Resist the temptation, at all costs. Fragmentation of data, processes, and culture will surely follow.

One might ask why such a decision needs to be taken at the start of the improvement program, when the model calls for definition and institutionalization of organization level processes at Level 3 of the CMM. This is done because, at some point in the organization's maturity cycle, definition and implementation of organization level processes will be required. If processes are in such disarray that they are in need of an overhaul, it will take less effort to define and institutionalize them at the organization level, in preparation for advancement to Level 3. This mindset itself demonstrates mature thinking and sets the organization on its way to process maturity. The organization should not just focus on the current CMM level it is trying to achieve or to assess itself to, but rather, what it can do to position itself for higher levels of maturity.

CMM-Based Improvement Program

Next comes the mundane but important task of defining and refining the organization's processes. Key metrics need to be defined, after a decision is taken on when they must be collected within the processes.

For an organization progressing to CMM Level 2, it is sufficient to define a set of processes that will be followed within each project group. However, in preparation for CMM Level 3, it is wise to spend time and effort determining all possible variations of the process and determining which allowable variations will be utilized in different circumstances. This activity readies the organization for an important key process area at CMM Level 3 called integrated software management. For example, a process followed by projects using a spiral life cycle model and object technology may be different from a process followed by projects that follow a traditional waterfall life cycle model. All such life cycle models and supporting processes must now be defined, refined, and key process metrics identified.

Once the processes are defined, they must be rolled out across the projects/organization. Process rollout generally includes activities such as training personnel in the use of the process, migrating all projects to the use of the process, determining which projects shall be grandfathered, determining exception handling for those projects that may need an undefined variation of the process, and so forth.

The key process area, software quality assurance (SQA) at Level 2 of the CMM, provides a strategy for SQA engineers to effectively ensure deployment and successful usage of the defined process.

Determining the success of a CMM-based improvement program necessitates the careful and consistent collection of key metrics and their continued analysis to control process implementation and institutionalization, to determine process efficiencies, and to rollout process changes. If key metrics are defined, collected and analyzed at every step, they will help determine the organization's readiness to proceed to the next CMM maturity level.

Every maturity level to be attained must be managed as a full-stream project, with goals, plans, schedules, and metrics. The management's continuous attention, monitoring, and support will not only facilitate rollout of the project, it will also communicate the importance of the effort, which will help to guarantee its success.

SUMMARY

Besides the Baldrige criteria, there are other widely accepted organizational assessment models that can be used to identify strategic opportunities. The European Foundation for Quality Management (EFQM) is similar in structure and application to the Baldrige model. It requires the use of a formal written assessment and use of trained examiners to determine the strengths and opportunities of an organization. This model is widely accepted throughout Europe but is based upon the Baldrige criteria. The SEI [Software] Capability Maturity Model (SEI/CMM) was developed for the US Government to assess software contractors because these types of companies and products were unlike other products and services it used. Although CMM can be used by any type of organization to assess performance and identity deficiencies, due to its focus on process management, it is best suited to software development organizations. The use of this model requires a thorough understanding of the criteria, and the use of trained team members to assess the breadth, depth, and alignment of an organization's processes, process controls, and internal measurements that lead to desired performance results. The scope of CMM is such that it does not explore all areas of the organization that support software development.

In the opinion of the authors, either one of these models is an acceptable alternative to the Baldrige model.

REFERENCES

(1) The European Foundation for Quality Management (EFQM), Brussels Representative Office, Avenue des Pleiades 15, 1200 Brussels, Belgium, Tel: +32-2 775 35 11, Fax: +32-2 775 35 35, Email: info@efqm.org,http://www.efqm.org, or P.O. Box 6386, NL-5600 HJ Eindhoven, The Netherlands, Stichtingenregister Eindhoven no. 41091319.

(2) Stephen H. Kann, "Metrics and Models in Software Quality Engineering," Second Edition, Published by Addison-Wesley, Boston, Massachusetts, USA, 2003.

(3) United States Department of Commerce, Technology Administration, National Institute of Standards and Technology, Baldrige National Quality Award Program, Administration Building, Room A635, 100 Bureau Drive, Stop 1020, Gaithersburg, Maryland, 20899-1020, USA. http://www.nist.gov

(4) The European Foundation for Quality Management (EFQM), Brussels Representative Office, Avenue des Pleiades 15, 1200 Brussels, Belgium, Tel: +32-2 775 35 11, Fax: +32-2 775 35 35, Email: info@efqm.org, http://www.efqm.org, or P.O. Box 6386, NL-5600 HJ Eindhoven, The Netherlands, Stichtingenregister Eindhoven no. 41091319.

PREPARING THE ORGANIZATION FOR CHANGE

To quote an anonymous author, "Change is inevitable except from a vending machine." Most individuals and organizations do not readily embrace change. Often, they take steps to avoid it. In many cases, individuals expend more energy resisting change, without realizing that it would take lesser energy to just change. It is human nature to accept status quo and feel uncomfortable about the unknown state brought on by change. A plethora of research exists on the topic of change and change management. Thousands of consultants are employed because of the inevitable and constant need for effective change management in organizations. And within organizations, effective change agents are desired commodities. This chapter will attempt to summarize some of this research but is not intended to explore in great depths all the behavioral research and techniques involved with organizational change.

LEADERSHIP COMMITMENT FOR CHANGE

As cited in the previous chapters, leadership commitment for an organizational activity, including change, is a key ingredient to effectively managing an organization. Leaders must be *actively* engaged and "walk the talk." Leaders should create or foster a culture where change, spurned by continuous improvement, is expected, and desired behaviors are rewarded. Leaders also need to assign and support effective change agents within an organization and hold key members within the organization responsible and accountable for achievement of results and continuous improvement. Status quo should not be tolerated.

The old adage "manage change or change management" cannot be more true. Unfortunately, most organizations, and people, don't deal with change particularly well. In addition to leading by example and supporting change within an organization, leaders need to help create an environment where the need for change is understood by everybody. Sometimes, this is communicated in a crisis mode, such as by an organization in dire financial straits and about to go out of business. By this time, it is probably too late to change. And the key stakeholders—employees, shareholders, communities, and so forth—will hold the leaders accountable for not having made the necessary changes to keep the organization viable and successful.

As will be discussed later in this chapter, leaders need to create or reinforce a culture that promotes change. Employees will constantly invoke the "WIIFM" adage—"What's In It For Me?" Leaders, working with their change agents, need to help the entire organization understand the need for change and the impact it will have on all individuals and parts of the organization. One way of doing this is by estimating the magnitude for change.

Change agents within an organization are rare yet desired entities. They must effectively implement changes throughout the organization, knowing that they will face resistance from every quarter. Change agents must serve as extensions of the senior management. The typical attributes change agents must possess include an ability to get things done by others, respect for and by the organization, and demonstrated history of achieving results and meeting commitments. Six Sigma Black Belts are taught change management as part of their overall training and make acceptable change agents in most cases. They identify new ways of performing old operations and implement these changes in various parts of an organization.

ESTIMATING THE MAGNITUDE FOR CHANGE

In most organizations, change occurs on a regular basis. However, its magnitude varies and, in many cases, organizations do not notice the changes that have taken place. Most large organizations manage change through periodic reorganizations or restructuring. This is depicted in Figure 5.1.[1] Organizations may restructure themselves every 12, 18, 24, or 36 months. Once they change, the new structure and behaviors settle for a period of time while everyone gets accustomed to the new structure. This stepwise approach to change is depicted by the stepping stone line in Figure 5.1. Gradually, the changes become more and more frequent and larger and more radical, or the organization will become less suited for the business environment. However, since the environment is acknowledged to be changing exponentially (the curved line in Figure 5.1), such an approach means the organization will always lag behind the ideal situation. The employees are sure to be frustrated by the tumultuous, periodic changes.

Another approach to change is continuous, depicted by the straight line in Figure 5.1. Perhaps an organization views the useful life of its technological base as 10 or 15 years, and depreciates and

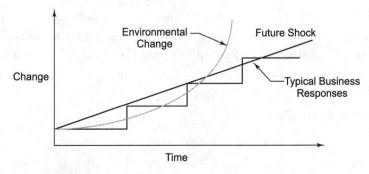

Fig. 5.1 The Change Curve—Elements of Change

replenishes the technological base accordingly. Perhaps an organization invests in a week or two of training each year, and relies on it to keep employees "up to speed." Perhaps an organization relies on the marketing strategy of "milking" mature products rather than rapid product innovation. All of these views will lead to a constant rate of change of 10 to 15 percent every year. This rate of change is guaranteed to eventually lead to mediocre organizational performance that ensures that the organization significantly lags behind the business environment.

If the environment is changing exponentially and organizations are changing slowly, in a stepwise or gradual fashion, facing future shock is inevitable. Often, the reality check takes the form of a merger or acquisition. Sometimes, the future shock takes the form of corporate bankruptcy. In some cases, the future shock takes the form of radical downsizing to hang on to one or two "core competencies." And, often, the future shock is marked by a significant decline in stock price with investors losing confidence in an organization. But if an organization pursues an appropriate strategy, the future shock may never happen.

Change, or expectations for change, can come to an organization through many different means. Some examples include:

Customer Expectations

Customers are dynamic and always changing. As individuals, we expect new products and services to be better and faster than the previous models or versions. We expect better service and technical support. Our expectations are continually increasing, as new levels of performance become the norm. Consumers do not expect product capability and service to decline. To meet these rising expectations, businesses must continually improve and innovate at a rate at least equal to the increase in customer expectations.

Technological Change

The rate of change in technology continues to accelerate. No longer are there "high technology" businesses; all businesses are directly affected by rapid technological change. Customers expect a new personal computer to have a faster processing speed, more memory, higher resolution, and better software. These expectations are uniform across almost all product and service industries. The Internet has changed the way business and support services are conducted. And there are certain to be big changes in the consumer use of the Internet when web TV becomes more widespread. The only thing certain is that there will be new and currently unavailable technological advances that will be in widespread use in five years.

According to the survey of CEOs, conducted by the US Department of Commerce, the second most critical issue in North America and Europe was dealing with rapid technological change.[2.] This was the most frequently identified issue in Asia. The issue of technological change included both rapid change in products as well as underlying systems. The implication is that functional life cycles have become shorter and shorter. For example, an old 486 computer with a Windows 3.1 operating system may still perform as well as it did in 1995, but it surely has been functionally obsolete for years.

Global Competition

The rate of growth of international trade among industrialized economies has been twice the rate of domestic economic growth for years. The issues that concerns CEOs today are related to globalization and global competition.[3] According to the survey conducted on behalf of the US Department of Commerce, many CEOs felt that within the next decade, foreign competition would pose a serious threat to their companies. The reason is that customers have a wide array of product and services to choose from. Country of origin of a product is less and less of a concern to customers and is often unknown. In fact, many "foreign" products have a higher domestic value-added content than traditional "domestic" products. Customers select from the products of the very best global suppliers, guaranteeing tough, global competition in all major economies.

Never before has it been easier to do business on an international basis. Companies specialized in dealing with customer, tariff, and shipping issues make the process of delivering goods and services to another country possible for organizations of any size. Many marketing plans being put in place today are global in nature. The ease of doing business internationally has spurned global competition in virtually every market segment.

Customization and Niche Players

Customers are demanding more and more customized products and services, forcing suppliers to produce more customized products that fit a customer's specific needs. This change in customer requirement is forcing organizations to change their productive processes to become more flexible and adaptable. There are many more "niche" markets (and market players) that larger organizations have trouble adapting to. Economic order quantities are not driven by a formula in an economics book; production levels are driven by customer demand that can change quickly.

Workforce Demographics

Workforce issues are a major challenge for most organizations. The mediocrity of the education system makes hiring and keeping good workers difficult. The industrialized economies all have aging populations, with many countries significantly older than the US. Employees are working and living longer. Older employees expect, and often demand, a different work environment. But the rapid technological changes often result in equally rapid knowledge obsolescence, resulting in the need to create new skill sets among employees. Continual learning is an often overlooked, or underestimated, factor in employee development. And the issues of workforce diversity never seem to go away.

Complicating all of this is the fact productivity improvements, particularly in manufacturing of all types, have led to a dramatically reduced workforce for most businesses. Stated simply, it takes fewer people to produce more products and services. An individual's career track may change direction frequently during his or her lifetime, with several job changes. But as skill requirements change with changes in technology, products, and services, finding the right people has never been more challenging. Skill acquisition and development is a key challenge for any organization, and just when an organization thinks it has the right skills on hand or planned, changes in the economy, industry, market, or customer requirements demand that a new set of skills be acquired. Collectively, these and other environment changes, present a major challenge for all organizations. Determining the magnitude for change requires deep research by the organization so that it does not underestimate its need and capacity for change.

MANAGING RESISTANCE TO CHANGE

Organizations need to be productive and practical in order to compete and survive. Organizations are made up of people—with feelings, aspirations, and fears. When the human side of the organization is well taken care of, change and success will occur. People can accomplish nearly anything if the desire and will exceeds their apprehensions.

There are fundamental reasons why individuals resist change. It is human nature. Some of these reasons are:

- **Inertia.** People are afraid that change will disrupt and slow down current levels of performance.

- **Habit.** People are used to doing things a certain way. The adages "old habits are tough to break" or "you can't teach an old dog new tricks" certainly apply.

- **Resource limitations.** There is never enough time or people to change what is being done today.

- **Threat to power or influence.** Certain individuals feel that they have control over the way things currently operate and change will eliminate their power or influence.

- **Fear of the unknown.** People get comfortable doing things a certain way and the fear of doing things differently or the impact it might have on them cause them to resist change.

- **Social influence and social information processing.** Change agents and change adopters are a minority in any organization. There is always power in numbers. People resist change because others do.

Change agents need to understand some fundamental techniques to overcome resistance to change. These include:

- Clarify the importance and urgency for the need to change.

- Foster the appropriate level of involvement and commitment throughout the organization. Leadership needs to stand behind the need for change.

- Provide facilitation and support to deploy the change throughout the organization, in the most effective and efficient manner.

- Identify and address individual differences in receptiveness to change.

- Address WIIFM issues.

Change agents need to help individuals in the organization accept and manage change. For instance, a change agent can talk to individuals in the organization and explain to them that change is all around and that it impacts our lives on a daily basis. The change agent will encounter a number of reactions to change that have been categorized as follows:

1. Bystanders, or those who are reluctant to get involved, wait to see if another will take the lead, and wait for others to adopt change before following.

2. Victims strongly resist change and feel angry or depressed about the need to change. They isolate themselves from others and will not ask for help. They prefer to go back to the old ways of doing things and, given the chance, will instantly revert back.

3. Change critics actively look for reasons why the change will not work. They challenge the appropriateness of change and go out of their way to demonstrate that the current way of doing things is better than the proposed way.

4. Technical resistors, or those who question all the technical details and reasons for the change, feel inept in the face of change because of new or different technology. They often recruit others to help resist the change.

5. Political or organizational resistors equate change to the loss of power. They strongly defend the status quo. Political or organizational resistors feel a strong sense of ownership and pride towards the existing system and resist anything "not invented here."

Change agents need to understand the types of individuals they will be faced with when introducing change and must take steps to address the subsequent reactions. They need to look for ways to minimize negative reactions, openly accept resistance and criticism, form relationships while moving through change, and ask others to help them implement change. Change agents will find early adopters and supporters along the way. Often, these individuals are tired of the old way and are looking for a better way. They just need direction and encouragement on how to change.

Some techniques that can help change agents implement change and address resistance include:

- Identify the need for change and the consequences of not changing.
- Hold regular meetings to give visibility to change.
- Analyze who will lose what as a result of the change.
- Talk about change in terms of the current environment and constraints.
- Provide the overall plan to execute the change.
- Let people know how their behaviors and attitudes will have to change and the consequences of not changing.
- Set clear goals, output objectives, expectations, deadlines, and establish feedback systems.

Techniques the change agent should avoid include:

- Punishing or discouraging employees from asking questions or expressing concerns or uncertainty.
- Assigning others the responsibility to plan and lead change.
- Oversimplify the change or its demands.
- Scrap the plan for one that seems less disruptive.
- Threaten disciplinary actions as a way to get people on board.

To understand how to manage resistance to change, it is important to first understand the dynamics in the change continuum. Figure 5.2 illustrates the four stages in any change continuum.

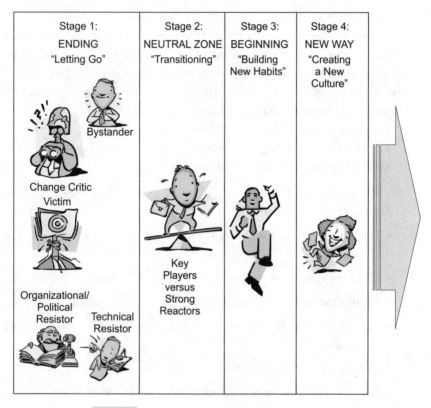

Fig. 5.2 Four Stages of a Change Continuum

Stage 1: The ENDING Stage

In this stage, people are in the process of letting go of their old habits and ways of performing but need encouragement and leadership. Ways to lead others during this step include:

- Make sure that individuals understand the scope and impact of the change.

- Identify what individual reactions are to the change and, based on this knowledge, help change their convictions.

- Tell them what the goals are and what the new expectations are.

- Ask them what their losses will be—either perceived or real— and address these concerns.

- Ask them what they believe are the expected gains.

- Identify the key players and strong reactors. Predict and prepare for how they will react.

- Set clear goals, output objectives, expectations, deadlines, and establish feedback systems.

When the organization is in the Ending stage, the change agent should:

- Start holding regular meetings with those affected to give visibility to the need for change as well as status of the change.

- Analyze who will lose what as a result of the change.

- Carefully prepare how to sell the problem that is prompting the change.

- Talk about the change in terms of current work and constraints.

- Provide the overall plan to execute the change.

- Let people know how their behavior and attitudes will have to change.

But,

- Do not assign the responsibility of planning and leading the change to someone other than the change agent.

- Do not oversimplify the change or its demands.

Stage 2: The NEUTRAL ZONE

When employees are in the neutral zone, the change agent must help them make the transition to the new way of doing things. This is often referred to as the "transition stage." In this stage, most of the organization has accepted the need for change and is ready to move on. Ways to lead others during this step include:

- Assess the "critical mass" of the group to ensure strong reactors have let go and key players have signed on.

- Reinforce the need for change and its benefits by meeting those who are affected.

- Ask others for ideas on how to make the transition smoother.

- Help individuals channel their energy into creative application of the process, to the benefit of the organization and its customers.

- Provide direction and specific assignments to complete the change.

When the organization is in the neutral zone, the change agent should:

- Re-channel energy into making the change happen smoothly.
- Encourage people to imagine a positive future.
- Create a sense of security in the future.
- Set clear goals, output objectives, expectations, deadlines, and establish feedback systems.

But,

- Do not punish individuals for asking questions or expressing concern or uncertainty.
- Do not scrap the plan for one that seems less disruptive.

Stage 3: The NEW BEGINNINGS Stage

In this stage, people seem to be making new "beginnings" and building new habits. Most of the organization has accepted the change. Ways to lead others during this stage include:

- Determine how many people or what percentage of the organization knows how to do the work the new way, has accepted the need for the change, and has made the new way a habit.
- To identify early wins and successes, meet with people to review how the improved change is performing.
- Constantly reinforce the expectations and the results as a way to sustain new habits.
- Celebrate progress and achievement.

When the organization is in the new beginnings stage, the change agent should:

- Provide coaching, training, and reinforcement on the right way to do the work.
- Get out of the way once people begin to demonstrate that they accept the change.

But,

- Do not accidentally or unintentionally reward "old" behaviors.
- Do not threaten disciplinary action as a way to get people on board.

Stage 4: The NEW WAY Stage

In this final stage in the change management continuum, people have adopted the new way, of doing things. The pervasive use of the new process makes this part of the organization's culture. Ways to lead others during this stage include:

- Get out of the way and let the organization function.
- Follow up with people to review how the improved change is performing in comparison to the old way of doing things.
- Monitor and report results after the change, comparing new performance against past performance.
- Celebrate.

When the organization is in the new way stage, the change agent's job is done. Responsibility and accountability for sustaining the new way should be turned over to management to monitor, measure, and manage. The employees in the organization should be rewarded for sustaining this new behavior with consequences for reverting back to the old way of doing things.

CREATING A FRAMEWORK TO SUPPORT CHANGE

Most organizational behavior textbooks illustrate a very simple behavior change model which suggests that, to achieve change, an organization must *unfreeze* old behaviors, *move* to new behaviors, and *refreeze* the new behaviors. This model suggests that the organization needs to modify its culture so as to accept the change and make it painful to revert back to the old way. An assessment of the organization should be conducted to determine the readiness for change. There must be acceptance and alignment by all key players in the organization. There are five broad categories that must be in place to support change in the organization.

Leadership, Commitment and Structure

The leaders of the organization must foster a culture that allows change to effectively take place throughout the organization. The organization must be *committed* to the need for change, and *structured* in the way of strategy, goals must support a culture of change. For instance, under the guise of continuous improvement, leadership should visibly and verbally support an environment focused on continuous improvement, supported by a formal strategy and goals that state the organization will constantly evaluate ways to get better over time.

Resources

Most change efforts require *resources* of some type. At the extreme, changes could require significant capital investment. Or, the required resources could be more modest for training employees in new skills. The allocation of resources is usually a good indicator of the manage-ment's commitment to change. This extends to the assignment of and support to an effective change agent. Without the commitment of adequate and required resources, change will not occur.

Skills

If employees are asked to change their behavior as part of an organization change, the employees must have the *skills* necessary to carry out the new behaviors. This implies that an assessment has been made of the required skills. The results of the assessment must be compared to the existing skills to identify training and development needs.

Incentives and Consequences

"What gets measured gets managed" is a well-known axiom, so is, "What gets rewarded gets done." The organization needs to develop *incentive* schemes so that employees embrace changes or the new ways of doing things. If incentives for change are not present, the rate of change is slower or zero. People should be rewarded for demonstrating new behaviors, this will help institutionalize the change and reinforce desired behaviors. For instance, if the change requires employees to acquire new skills, there should be some incentive for doing so. Conversely, *consequences* should exist for not changing. An example of this could be that the change drives significantly better performance results that are not achievable using the old method or process.

Action Plans

The fifth element that must be present is an action plan—a formalized approach to change. If a change is proposed or an edict given, there is little that will happen unless there are formal plans to support the change. A detailed action plan for deployment and implementation of a change will provide a road map for the organization to assess how well the change is being implemented and accepted.

The organization, through its change agent, should assess the readiness of the organization for change. In addition to assessing the five areas above, the assessment should also consider the availability and existence of required resources, complexity of the change, the time line for the change to be implemented, identification and readiness of responsibilities throughout the organization, and development of

Characteristic	Readiness for Change			Recommended Actions
	Low	Moderate	High	
Senior Leadership				
Corporate Strategies				
Goals and Objectives				
Organizational Structure				
Financial Resources				
Information Technology				
Accounting Systems				
Human Resources				
Functional Area Managers				
• Employees				
• Union				
Supply Chain				
Suppliers, Vendors, Partners				
Sales and Marketing				

Fig. 5.3 Organizational Assessment of Readiness for Change

a formal deployment strategy. Examples of checklists for assessing organizational readiness for change are shown in Figures 5.3 and 5.4.[4]

Characteristic	Support for Change			Recommended Actions
	Low	Moderate	High	
RESOURCE ALLOCATION				
• Capital Investment				
• Implementation Expenses				
• Direct and Indirect Labor				
COMPLEXITY				
• Localized Projects				
• Moderate Projects				
• Large Projects				
TIME LINE				
• Short term				
• Moderate term				
• Long term				
AREA OF RESPONSIBILITY				
• Individual				
• Functional Manager				
ROLLOUT STRATEGY				
• Full Rollout				
• Phase In				
ACTION PLAN DEVELOPED				

Fig. 5.4 Assessment of Requirements for Change

SUMMARY

Change in an organization is inevitable. It is brought on by a number of factors including customer demands, technological advancements, competition, customization of products and services, and changes in workplace demographics, among other things. People will resist change. It is human nature. Change agents can combat this by understanding the factors that impact the four stages of a change continuum, and the behavior of resistors. Finally, an organization needs to create a framework to reinforce desired change behaviors across the organization. Desired behaviors and outcomes should be rewarded and it should be painful not to change or to return to old ways of doing things. Change agents need to assess the readiness of an organization for change before proceeding with detailed plans to deploy a major change initiative. The five elements needed to ensure organizational readiness for change include leadership; commitment and structure; resources; skills; incentives and consequences; and action plans.

REFERENCES

(1) "Customer Centered Six Sigma: Linking Customers, Process Improvement, and Financial Results," ASQ Quality Press, Milwaukee, Wisconsin, USA, 2001 by Earl Naumann and Steven H. Hoisington.

(2) Ibid.

(3) http://www.quality.nist.gov, Baldrige National Quality Program, National Institute of Standards and Technology, Technology Administration, United States Department of Commerce, Administration Building, Room A600, 100 Bureau Drive, Stop 1020, Gaithersburg, Maryland, USA 20899-1020, "Baldrige: A Global Approach for a Global Economy," August 2000.

(4) "Customer Centered Six Sigma: Linking Customers, Process Improvement, and Financial Results," ASQ Quality Press, Milwaukee, Wisconsin, USA, 2001 by Earl Naumann and Steven H. Hoisington.

ALIGNING THE ORGANIZATION FOR TRANSFORMATION

BALANCED SCORECARD AND ITS ADVANTAGES

Traditionally, at least until the last decade or so, most organizations relied upon using financial measures as the index of their performance and tried to deliver shareholder value by developing astute operational plans that focused on driving financial numbers (e.g., gross margin, revenue, cost per asset ratio, etc). The end result of such efforts invariably led to financial success over the short term. However, to sustain that success over a longer period, executives realized they had to bring about a change in the use of those methods.

The switch to a new paradigm that requires organizations to now focus on both financial and non-financial measures linked to the strategy of that organization has met with resounding success in the recent past. This has been the underlying principle in the evolution of the Balanced Scorecard approach first enunciated by Robert

Kaplan and David Norton in the early 1990s.[1] While most people are familiar with financial measures, the typical non-financial measures are those related to customers (e.g., customer satisfaction, customer complaints, employee turnover, employee satisfaction, productivity, etc.). The Balanced Scorecard, first introduced in Chapter 2, complements financial measures of past performance with measures of the drivers of future performance. Kaplan and Norton refined this concept to view organizational performance from four perspectives: Financial, Customer, Internal Business Process, and Learning and Growth (Figure 6.1).[2]

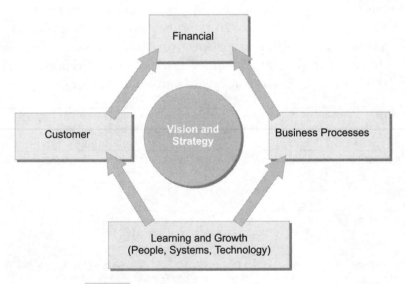

Fig. 6.1 Balanced Scorecard Perspectives

BALANCED SCORECARD—THE CONCEPT

Traditional scorecards have relied on the use of measuring the financial metrics of any organization. While this has stood the test of time so far, most executives are now realizing the need to shift to a focus on tracking non-financial measures in addition for sustained market leadership. Financial measures such as ROI, EPS, gross margin, and so forth are lagging indicators. The key to long-term success is dependent on how well the organization understands their customers and their requirements, how strong is the alignment of its people with the strategies of the organization and how well the operational processes are structured in the organization that is tuned to customer needs. Measurement on these dimensions (leading indicators) coupled with the ones on financial dimensions (lagging indicators) provides the necessary balance and hence the Balanced Scorecard.[3]

Schiemann and Lingle[4] put a spin on the above definition and proposed six perspectives rather than four (Figure 6.2). They demonstrated that this was a workable proposal, given the fact that in today's world, the number of virtual organizations have steadily increased the importance of alliance partners and suppliers for effective strategy implementation. As a result, they added a Partners/Suppliers category and another one on Environment to complement the basic four perspectives and asserted further that they were "yet to find an organization that cannot be represented in its key elements by performance goals within these six areas."

Market	Focus on customers, potential customers, competitors' customers, and other customers
Financial	Focus on shareholders/stakeholders in the business
People	Associates/Employees
Operations	Operational Process—those that translate customer requirements into products/services
Environment	Focus on Environment, Health, and Safety, and regulatory requirements and key communities of interest
Partners/Suppliers	Focus on Suppliers/Partners/Distributors on the supply chain

Fig. 6.2   Key Performance Measurement Perspectives

Strategy and the Balanced Scorecard

Several organizations are moving into the realm of "measurement management" that appears to give them a sense of where they are relative to where they should be. We have also seen such scorecards identify measures that are pertinent to an organization's stakeholder set (e.g., customers, employees, community, etc.). These scorecards are known either as KPI (Key Performance Indicator) scorecards or stakeholder scorecards. Many of the organizations that employ the Baldrige assessment approach construct scorecards as a response to Item 2.1 of the Baldrige criteria. The deficiency in such scorecards, however, is that they do not give an organization a feel of how "balance" will be achieved. Balance will come once those measures are linked to the strategy of the organization. That is, when the scorecard becomes a Balanced Scorecard.

Importance and Relevance of Strategy

Various current initiatives such as Key Result Area (KRA) programs, Annual Operating Plans (AOP), and objective setting exercises are found to be typical number-crunching efforts rather than frameworks to align, plan, act, review, and improve organizational performance. Key factors, identified by a survey of Chief Financial Offices (CFOs) that contribute to the failure of strategy implementation are[5]:

- Only 60% of executives, 40% of middle management and 5% of line employees understand the vision and strategy of the organization.

- 69% of managers do not perceive any significant role of strategic planning process in overall success.

- 57% of managers cannot perceive a link between the long-range strategy and annual budgets.

- 85% of managers spend less than 15% of their time making strategic decisions/redirecting the organization.

- Only 34% of executives, 15% of middle management, and 5% of line employees have incentives linked to strategy.

Some additional statistical information reproduced from the same source provides further evidence that the importance given to strategy is not as favorable as it should be (see Figures 6.3 and 6.4). Suffice to say, from the above discussion, that strategy development and deployment in most organizations is a one-off affair, at least in the way it is used as a cornerstone around which a strategic measurement system is conceived and deployed throughout the organization.

Source: CFO Magazine Survey

Fig. 6.3   Strategy and Its Relevance in Organizations

The Vision Barrier

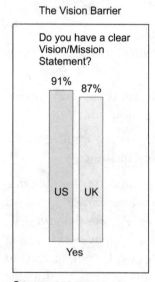

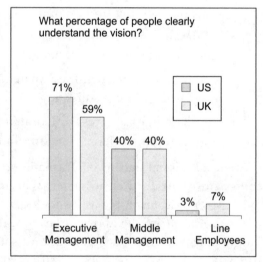

Source: CFO Magazine Survey

Fig. 6.4   Strategy and Linkage to Individual Performance Management

The Cause and Effect Relationship—the Key to an Effective Balanced Scorecard

In an earlier section, we discussed the need to link the strategy of the organization to the set of measures it considers most important. This lends a balanced look to its measurement system. One other aspect that needs to be considered is the cause and effect relationship between and amongst those measures. In the opinion of the authors, this has been the biggest differentiator in the experience of organizations that embraced this concept. Such a relationship, explained in Figure 6.5, underscores the fact that while the organization needs to work on only those measures that are tied to its strategies, the cause and effect relationship further helps to refine those measures in that:

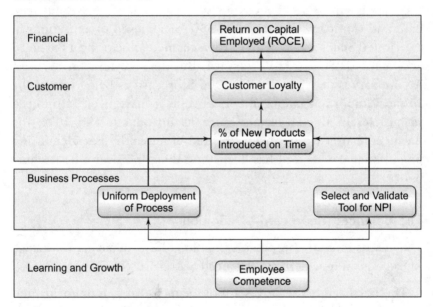

Fig. 6.5 Cause and Effect Relationship

- The measures are now only a handful (e.g., they are the ones "needed" by the organization as opposed to the "nice to do" measures), and

- The measures provide a better understanding of the effect of one measure on the other. For example, if the measurement of employee satisfaction improves, what happens to the productivity and in turn its effect on "on time delivery" and other operational measurements, assuming these are some of the measures on the scorecard? The cause and effect relationship that links to the strategic objectives is sometimes referred to as strategy maps in scorecard parlance.[6] Strategy maps will be explained in more detail in a later section.

Thus, a Balanced Scorecard is built on two core concepts:

1. The measures need to be linked to the strategies of the organization and be in balance.

2. There is a need to establish a cause and effect relationship between the measures that then results in a strategic management system.

Initially adopted by a few select organizations, the idea has spread very rapidly. In its 1999 executive survey of management practices, Bain and Company reported that 55% of surveyed organizations in the United States and 45% in Europe claimed to be using a Balanced Scorecard (BSC).[7] The Harvard Business review, in its 75th Anniversary issue, cites the Balanced Scorecard as being one of the 15 most important management concepts to have been introduced via articles in the magazine. Since its introduction in 1992, the Balanced Scorecard has been featured in a wealth of academic and practitioner papers and has been the subject of several best selling books.[8]

The Balanced Scorecard—Definition

The discussions in the previous sections have taken us to a stage where we can now define a Balanced Scorecard (BSC):

The Balanced Scorecard is a tool for measuring, monitoring and tracking organizational performance on financial and non-financial dimensions. Additionally, the financial and non-financial measures need to be linked to and derived from the strategy(ies) of the organization.[9]

The scorecard provides an enterprise view of an organization's overall performance by integrating financial measures with other key performance indicators around customer perspectives, internal business processes, organizational growth, learning, and innovation. The BSC is not a static list of measures, but a framework for implementing and aligning complex programs of change and, indeed, for managing strategy-focused organizations.

The Balanced Scorecard Perspectives

As we discuss the implementation of the Balanced Scorecard, we would like to recall some of the concepts enunciated in the previous sections. The conventional governance, management, and performance review systems have focused primarily on the measures of financial performance. The Balanced Scorecard approach begins with the premise that financial measures alone are not sufficient to manage an organization. Financial measures tell the story of past events. They are not helpful in guiding the creation of future value through investments in customers, suppliers, employees, technology, or innovation.

The Balanced Scorecard complements measures of past performance (lagging indicators) with measures of the drivers of future performance (leading indicators). The objectives and measures of the scorecard are derived from an organization's vision and strategy. These objectives and measures provide a view of an organization's performance from four perspectives.

1. "Financial Perspective" focuses on the strategy for growth, profitability, and risk viewed from the perspective of the shareholder.

2. "Customer Perspective" focuses on the strategy for creating value and differentiation from the customer viewpoint.

3. "Internal Perspective" focuses on the strategic priorities for various key processes which create customer and shareholder satisfaction.

4. "Learning and Growth Perspective" focuses on the strategic priorities to create a climate that supports organization change, innovation, and growth.

Through the measures on the Balanced Scorecard, organizations can focus on how their business units create value for current and future customers. Organizations can also learn what investments in people, systems, and procedures are necessary to improve future performance. While retaining an interest in financial performance, the Balanced Scorecard clearly reveals the drivers of superior, long-term value and competitive performance. A properly constructed Balanced Scorecard, therefore, measures the strategy of the organization.

Ten Steps to Implement a Balanced Scorecard

Step 1: Build Consensus around Strategy

The senior leadership in an organization needs to first discuss the mission (the reason for its being), vision (where it wants to be), and strategy (how to get to where it wants to be), and arrive at a common understanding. This is akin to setting the stage so that the team can start work on the next step. Experience has shown that this, however, is easier said than done. The reasons are not far to seek.

The Chief Financial Officer (CFO) in an organization may think of a set of strategies that seem important from his or her perspective. The marketing and sales chief might come up with a list that he/she thinks contains the top few strategies. These may not necessarily be the same as the ones the CFO came up with. Hence, building consensus on the strategies at an organization-wide level such that the entire leadership team is on the same page could be a daunting task.

While no particular approach is ideal, a practical and a suggested methodology for building consensus is as follows:

A "How to" Approach on Consensus Building

The authors, while working with a mid-sized market leader in the Information Technology (IT) sector, created a forum called the Strategy Consensus Forum that consisted of all those who directly reported to the CEO, including the CEO. To begin with, the CEO presented to this forum his perception of the strategies. Each of the senior leaders then provided their own interpretation and, after a few iterations, a first pass of the organization's strategies were developed.

A typical process of strategy development is shown in Figure 6.6. Some fundamental steps for any strategy development process are:

- Collection of information and data on the current environment, stakeholder needs, competition, and internal performance.

- Analysis of market and competition, analysis of client/ customer relationships, and analysis of internal capability based on information collected (the Baldrige criteria Item 2.1 on "Strategy Development" covers in great detail the factors that need to be considered in the development of a strategy).[10]

- Additional SWOT analysis as described in Chapter 2

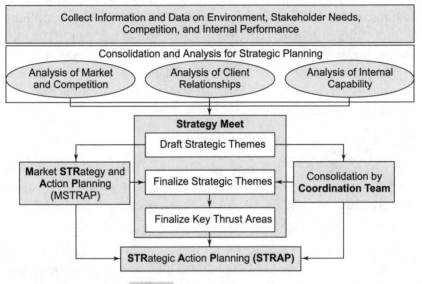

Fig. 6.6 Strategy Development

Next, this information was shared and communicated with the next level of the management. This meant two days of intense deliberations, spread across the globe. Called the "Strategy Meet," it was facilitated by the senior management through electronic and video conferencing. The first pass of the list of strategies arrived through the above steps were scrutinized. The outcome was a polished version, after factoring in all constraints as perceived by the management at this level. Several iterations at this level resulted in an agreed set of strategic themes that would be fed back to the senior leadership team. The net outcome of this process was a robust set of strategies that were accepted by the entire organization.

What has been described is perhaps a common sense approach, but to arrive at an agreement across the rank and file of an organization is perhaps a rarity. The statistical data discussed earlier reinforces this assertion further.

Having arrived at a consensus on the strategies, the senior leadership team drafted a list of strategic objectives that link and support the high level strategy.

Strategic objectives, key business drivers, or critical success factors are some of the phrases used to describe the objectives and action plans that support the strategies. In the end, the organization must recognize those few, most important objectives that it must work on to differentiate itself in its target market for both the short and long term. Strategic objectives are less esoteric and, to realize the strategy, an organization must work on the objectives. For example, the organization could have a strategy to "delight the customer" and the strategic objectives could be to "increase customer satisfaction and reduce customer complaints."

Step 2: Synthesize Strategic Objectives

The first pass on the list of strategic objectives that were derived from the previous step can be finalized at this step. Before synthesis begins the organization can run a sanity check on how meaningful and robust are the strategic objectives.

Figures 6.7 and 6.8 illustrate examples of how to apply a sanity check or validate the objectives—from a human resources and customer perspective—by asking some basic questions that will help everybody in the organization understand the total implications of meeting strategic objectives. Based on the common understanding of the mission, vision, and a set of strategic objectives, it is now necessary to synthesize them under each of the four perspectives of the Balanced Scorecard concept: Financial, Customer, Internal, and Learning. This is assuming the organization has chosen to work on the four-perspectives model rather than the six-perspectives version discussed earlier.

When working on the synthesis, it would be useful to split them into the four categories keeping the cause and effect relationship in mind. In Figure 6.5, we introduced the concept of the cause and effect relationship and how it is a key in the development of strategy maps.

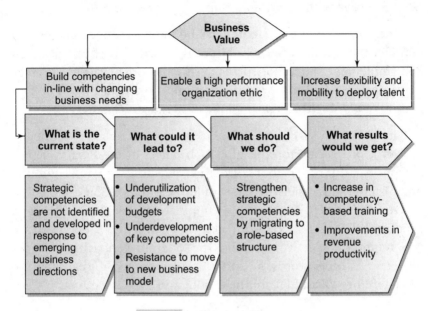

Fig. 6.7 Strategic Objectives

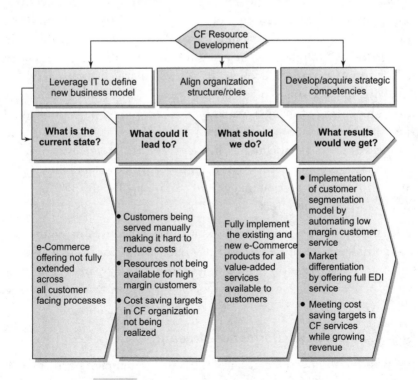

Fig. 6.8 Strategic Objectives: An Illustration

Step 3: Prepare the Strategy Map

To reiterate, it is important to understand the cause-effect relationship between the various strategic objectives in order to effectively align and implement the action plans across the organization. Strategy maps developed in the previous step are refined in this step. This may involve going through a couple of iterations (Figure 6.9).

For example, in Figure 6.9, the strategy to achieve profitable growth is one of the top five global objectives in the Financial (F1) perspective. In order to realize this objective, the question the organization must ask is: "What should the organization do to get to this desired state?" The answers, "Improve market share of chosen products" (F2) and "attain world class cost competitiveness" (F3), are two required objectives to help the organization achieve its F1 objective. In other words, F2 and F3 contribute to the realization of F1. Therefore F2 and F3 are the causes, and F1 is the effect.

This paradigm now allows the organization to take each of these objectives (e.g., F1, F2, and F3) and move into other perspectives. Continuing with the example, let's select F1 and see what might be the causes in the Customer perspective. "Retain profitable customers" (C1) appears to be a key area that needs a strong focus to help the organization achieve its F1. Similarly, if we select F2, "improve market share of niche products," C2 (acquire customers through existing offerings) would be the cause of F2. If we look at F3 (attain world class competitiveness), what this translates to in the Business Process perspective is in fact a set of objectives: "improve order management process" (B4), "improve process capability" (B5), and 'improve supplier management' (B6). So B4, B5, B6 are the causes and F3 is the effect.

It is, therefore, possible to look at other objectives in Figure 6.9 and complete the 'cause and effect' relationships for each. This step helps the organization to complete the strategy map that was developed in Step 2 as a first pass of the organization's strategic objectives.

Step 4: Select the Performance Measures

It is possible to now select a set of measures to manage performance against each of the strategic objectives developed in the earlier step.

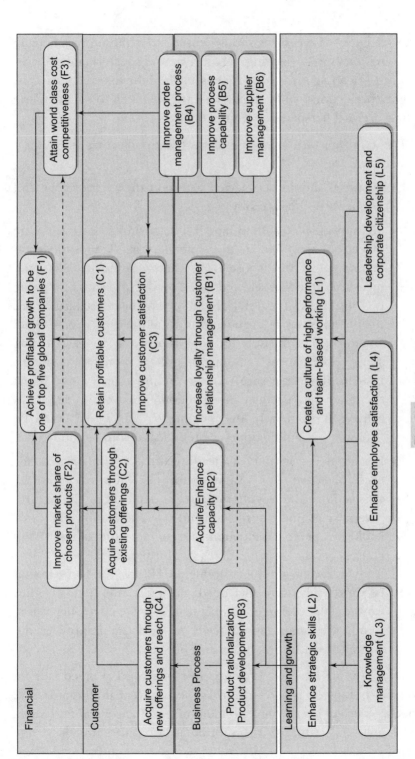

Fig. 6.9 Strategy Map

The selection of measures should ensure that there are adequate outcome measures (lagging measures) and performance driver measures (leading measures). Against each of the selected measures, targets, projections, and comparisons are tabulated to complete the four scorecard perspectives (Figure 6.10).

The following are some useful tips when selecting the performance measures:

- Measures should be selected based on their importance and not because they are easy.

- Measures picked should have a linkage and a bearing on the objectives identified in the strategic map. For example, in Figure 6.9, if we choose L2 (enhance strategic skills), the measure should be selected based on the impact it has on the two objectives L1 and B3. L1 and B3 have been established per the previous step as the effect and L2 as the cause. So, to select an appropriate measure for L2, it is probably no use selecting a measure such as "amount of dollars spent on training." Instead, if the measure was, say, "number of training hours spent on new product introduction," this may greatly help achieve B3. Similarly, the measure to achieve L1 could be "number of training hours spent on leadership development."

- It is not necessary to pick a leading and a lagging measure for each objective. For example, for C3 (improve customer satisfaction), the lagging indicator is depicted in Figure 6.10, "overall customer satisfaction index." The leading indicator could be "percent reduction in customer complaints." What matters is the organization's performance on both these leading and lagging measurements. Hence, the focus should be on that measure that needs the most attention. In other words, if the customer complaint rate is showing a degrading trend, the organization needs to work on improving the customer satisfaction index and vice versa.

Target setting for each measure must be arrived at based on data and not because it is convenient. For example, if the organization chooses a target for the measurement of "number of training hours per employee," naturally it cannot be an arbitrary number or one

Sr.	Strategic Objectives	Performance Measures	2K3-2K4	2K6-2K7	Comp.
A	**Financial Perspective**				
F1	To achieve profitable growth to be amongst top five global companies	• Return on capital employed • PBIDT/sales • % Contribution of niche products	X% X% X%	Y% Y% Y%	Z% Z% Z%
F2	Improve market share of niche products for market leadership	• Market share (domestic) for niche products • Export as % of total sale	X% X%	Y% Y%	Z% Z%
F3	To attain cost competitiveness at world class levels	• % sale which is not cost competitive • Operating cost as % of contribution	XX% X%	YY% Y%	ZZ% Z%
B	**Customer Perspective**				
C1	Retain and increase share of customer business	• % Sale to key customers • % Contribution from key customers • Business share of key customers	X% X% X Rs	Y% Y% Y Rs	Z% Z% Z Rs
C2	Acquire new customers through improved customer value offerings and customer reach	• Revenue growth from new offerings • % Contribution on sale of new offerings • Market share in new markets	X Rs X% B%	Y Rs Y% C%	Z Rs A% Z%
C3	Improve customer satisfaction on identified critical attributes	• Overall customer satisfaction index	H%	G%	I%
C	**Business Process Perspective**				
B1	Enhance customer loyalty through improved customer relationship management	• Customer repurchase intention • % Sale through e-Commerce	U% H%	I% L%	K% M%
B2	To review product mix and enhance product range	• % Sales volume with negative contribution • Cumulative sales volume from new products	H% G Units	Nil K Units	G% J Units
B3	Improve cost effectiveness by enhancing efficiency and optimizing resource utilization	• Wage bill as % of value addition • Cost of quality • % Reduction in overhead	K% G Rs J%	N% K Rs K%	L% H Rs H%
D	**Learning and growth perspective**				
L1	Create a culture of high performance and team work	• % Officers rated as high performers • % of employees in active teams	J% N%	K% K%	L% J%
L2	Enhance strategic skills/competencies	• % Adherence to strategic training plan	H%	D%	S%
L3	Enhance employee well-being, motivation, and satisfaction	• Employee satisfaction index	K%	H%	N%

Fig. 6.10 The Scorecard

where the organization thinks it "feels" right. Training is an investment and there is a dollar value associated with it. Instead, the organization needs to know the amount that has been spent over the past few years, and the return on its training investment. Then, the organization needs to determine what it needs and can afford. At the same time, it would be beneficial to gather some competitive or benchmark data for comparison. If the organization has an objective of employing the best skills in the industry, its training investment needs to reflect this.

The following are some useful guidelines in establishing targets:

- The purpose of defining targets is to communicate the expected level of performance, help create a focus on improvement, and set benchmarks and stretch expectations.

- In terms of criteria for defining targets, set only one target per measure that is quantifiable and ensure that it is clearly communicated.

- To set a target, derive performance expectations from overall goals (e.g., revenue expectations), benchmark with industry leaders, review past performance, and establish baselines and define targets over time.

Step 5: Select Strategic Initiatives

In order to achieve the targets determined against the strategic objectives, the organization has to undertake a set of strategic initiatives. For each of the strategic objectives and their corresponding measures, a set of initiatives need to be selected and an "initiative map" be prepared. An initiative map highlights the relationship between the strategic objectives and the initiatives. This is discussed in detail in the next chapter.

Step 6: Communicating the Balanced Scorecard

Communication by the senior leadership team that indicates the importance and relevance of the scorecard, why this approach was chosen over others methods, and how strategy is central to the working of the organization will be a resounding endorsement that will align the entire workforce. Simultaneously, it will send strong signals regarding the senior leadership's commitment and acceptance, and dispel the notion that this is not "a flavor of the month" program.

For communication to be effective, it is best to develop a formal communication plan. Such plans are always desirable for deployment of any kind of initiative, more so if the initiative implies a cultural shift and a paradigm change, such as in this case. A communication plan is a means to prepare and plan the communications efforts for any initiative undertaken by the organization. Knowing how much to communicate, when to communicate, and to whom to communicate comes through a well thought out communication plan.

A formal communication plan helps:

- keep communication focused.
- maintain consistency in communication.
- serve as a very important change management tool.
- in ensuring that all people (both internal and external) are effectively informed about the BSC initiative.
- prevent unwanted surprises (when the people involved hear about what's happening from someone outside the system).

The communication plan should contain details of all communication delivery mechanisms, their purpose, the targeted audience, the information content, and the person responsible for them. Figure 6.11 illustrates a communication plan for an IT company. The communication plan should also identify a means for assessing the effectiveness of the communication plan itself, such as a user survey to determine if employees received the desired communication.

Step 7: Cascading the Balanced Scorecard—(Figure 6.12)

The purpose of cascading the Balance Scorecard throughout the organization is to ensure complete alignment between the organizational measures at the top and individual business units/functions at the lower levels, down to individuals. Sometimes, this is referred to as the "line of sight alignment." An individual, therefore, works for an organization either in support of external customers or in support of internal customers. Interpreted

#	Communication Delivery Mechanisms	Purpose of Communication	Audience	Message of Communication	Delivered by?	Prepared by?	When
1	Home Page	1. Structure of BSC 2. Roles and responsibilities	All	Contains details regarding the need for BSC, benefits to the organization, etc.	Communication Group	Communication Group	Existing and is regularly updated
2	Newsletter	1. To create an awareness among the audience on the new initiatives undertaken by the organization. 2. To disseminate information on the status of the BSC	All	1. A high-level summary of the BSC initiative. 2. Updates since the last newsletter	Communication Group	Communication Group	Bi-monthly
3	Quarterly All-Hands Broadcast	1. Dissemination of performance of the organization 2. Corrective action plan for measures not on target	All	1. Scorecard results 2. Reasons for non-performance in some areas 3. Action plans to fix non-performance in specific areas	CEO	Communication Group	Every quarter following quarterly earnings report
4	Annual Performance Appraisal Process	1. Reinforce linkage of individual scorecards to BSC	All	1. Alignment– individual and organization scorecard 2. Compensation tie in to individual performance on the scorecard	HR chief	HR Group	Once in six months to coincide with mid-year and end-of-year reviews

Fig. 6.11 Communication Plan

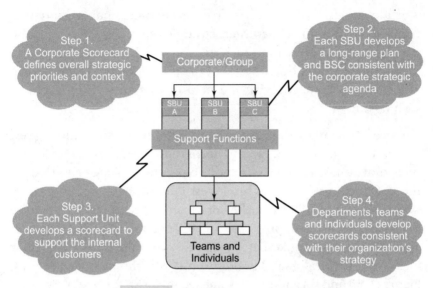

Fig. 6.12 Cascading the Scorecard

differently, what this means is that an individual delivers value to his or her group or department by way of working to meet its goals, which in turn have a bearing on the organizational goals. This is discussed in detail in the next section.

To facilitate the cascading process, it may be useful to think of a "governance model" such as the one shown in Figure 6.13. In fact, if the BSC initiative is managed as a formal project, which it should be, this model also helps to manage the project. In Figure 6.13, the program manager is the person who has the overall responsibility for implementation of the BSC across the organization. The core team

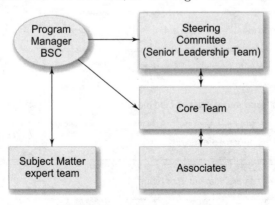

Fig. 6.13 Governance Model

is made up of representatives from each functional organization (e.g., marketing, manufacturing, customer support, HR, etc.). The steering committee is the top leadership in the organization, and their job is to review the progress of the project on an ongoing basis. The program manager, with the help of the core team, facilitates such meetings.

Once the scorecard measures have been finalized at the highest level in the organization, the core team representatives can work with their functional management and the program manager to cascade the BSC measures down to the lowest level of their organization. It will be the responsibility of the core team representative to finalize the measure for its appropriateness relative to his or her function and also be the spokesperson to work on the target for their measures. A typical goal flow-down process is shown in Figure 6.14. Figures 6.15 and 6.16 illustrate some examples of the goal flow down for a financial measurement and a customer measurement. The concept of Hoshin Planning, discussed in Chapter 9, is an example of how goals can be cascaded down the organization, and how department or individual goals can be developed to support the overall objectives and strategies of the organization.

1. Understand the metrics of Corporate Scorecard	**Meeting 1**
2. Understand metrics analyzed by core team	
3. Analyze current Performance Indicators (PIs)	
4. Brainstorm to identify probable set of PIs	
5. Select metrics and draft your scorecard	**Meeting 2**
6. Define proposed targets for selected metrics	
7. Discuss with concerned director	**Meeting 3**
8. Finalize and communicate to your team	**Meeting 4**

Fig. 6.14 The Goal Flow-Down Process

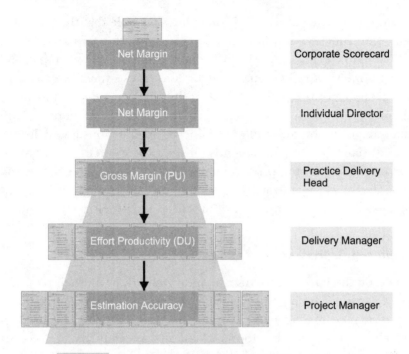

Fig. 6.15 Flow-Down Process Illustration: Financial Goal

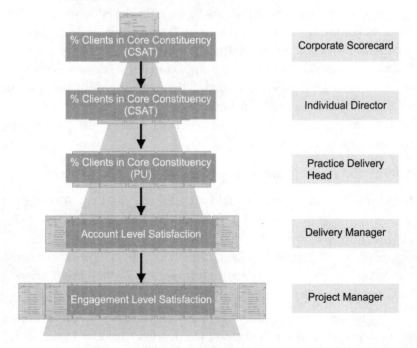

Fig. 6.16 Flow-Down Process Illustration: Customer Goal

In the cascade exercise, it is sometimes possible that the measures for some functions do not directly map to the top level scorecard. This might be the case with a support function, for example, the procurement organization. In such cases, those functions need to work on measures that satisfy their internal customers and allow them to be successful in meeting their goals. For example, if the manufacturing organization has a metric such as "on time delivery" and if that organization depends on the procurement organization for supplies, then the procurement organization would support the manufacturing organization's goal and, therefore, might implement a metric such as "the number of procured items delivered on time."

Step 8: Align Human Resource Aspects to the Balanced Scorecard

Based on the Balanced Scorecard, individuals draw up their personal scorecards, which then integrate with the organization's performance management system. The scorecard can be used to develop personal development plans as well as to design compensation and incentive systems.

There are a number of factors to be considered when assessing and developing human resource requirements to support achievement of Balanced Scorecard objectives. Category 5 of the Baldrige criteria identifies some possible human resource requirements and considerations.[11] These include skills required to support the strategies, employee satisfaction, productivity, and adverse indicators of satisfaction such as absenteeism, employee turnover, and safety incidents.

Step 9: Set up a Strategic Feedback and Review System

Improvements in organizational performance can be achieved only if performance is reviewed continuously. This is done using the Balanced Scorecard. A review structure is designed using the Balanced Scorecard as the basic framework. The following are some useful tips to design a review structure, some of which are described in Category 1 of the Baldrige criteria[12]:

- The governance model described in Figure 6.13 can serve as a vehicle for not only the cascade process (discussed previously) but also for reporting and review.

- The core team representative would function as a conduit to facilitate information flow to and from the functional area that he or she represents.
- It may be useful to design a template that everyone in the organization could use for reporting and tracking. A template sample is shown in Figure 6.17.

Sr.	Performance Measure	Unit of Measure	Target 2002–2003		Actual Performance				Score 1–5 Scale	Visual Indicator		
			Minimum Level	Aspiration Level	Qtr 1	Qtr 2	Qtr 3	Qtr 4		R	Y	G
1	Relationship Value	60%										
a	Service Quality Metric											
b	Productivity Metric											
c	Schedule Metric											
d	Budget/Cost Metric											
2	Relationship Strength	20%										
a	Customer Satisfaction Metric											
b	Depth of Engagement Metric											
3	Future Value and Growth	20%										
a	Program Management Metric											
b	Technology Expertise Metric											
c	Domain Competence Metric											
	Total Score	100%										

Fig. 6.17 The Balanced Scorecard Template

- Before going too far, a review of the capability of the current information systems used to generate the information needed would be in order. It is not surprising that many IT systems don't work as planned to support a Balanced Scorecard of measurements.

- The program manager, in concert with the steering committee, can decide on the frequency of reporting. Reporting, with formal reviews every quarter, is a common practice. In some organizations, reporting and reviews are conducted monthly.

- A dashboard is a useful idea to serve as a status indicator of current performance. A green status means the metric is on track to meet the target, yellow means there is a potential risk of the metric not meeting the target, and red means the metric is in a critical state, warranting immediate attention.

- It is helpful to document the metric definitions on the scorecard so that there is no confusion and also to identify the executive owner for each metric at the senior leadership level.

Additional information regarding the format and conduct of performance reviews is discussed in Chapter 9.

Step 10: Sustain the Gains and Revisit the Scorecard Annually

Like any other initiative, the Balanced Scorecard needs management support. Strategies, priorities, and requirements constantly change, so the Balanced Scorecard needs to be reviewed at least annually to adjust the metrics and targets. The Balanced Scorecard is a living document and changes should be tightly managed.

Recap

To recap and to summarize, the above 10 steps have been summarized in Figure 6.18. Implementing a Balanced Scorecard involves a phased approach with meticulous change management. The first step is the definition phase. This phase usually takes three to four weeks and delivers the following results, which form the foundation for the later phases:

- Consensus on vision and future scenarios
- Articulation of key strategic objectives

- Performance metrics (Balanced Scorecard)
- Initiatives to meet strategic objectives

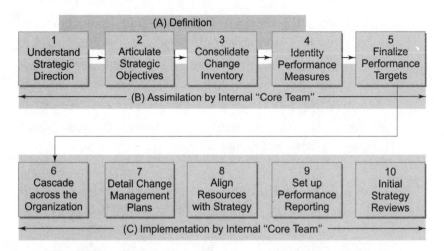

Fig. 6.18 Three Phases of Balanced Scorecard Implementation

The results of the definition phase are put into play to bring about the second phase—assimilation. This phase usually lasts four to six weeks. During this period, an internal core team socializes the process with all the key stakeholders and finalizes the elements of implementation.

The third phase is the implementation phase. Here, the internal core team deploys the process on an ongoing basis. It typically takes six to eight months to achieve a total blending of Balanced Scorecard processes that are aligned with and support key management systems.

Advantages of Implementing the Balanced Scorecard

To summarize, the implementation of the Balanced Scorecard through the steps defined above, provides the following benefits:

- It facilitates communication across the organization and enhances the understanding of vision and strategy.
- It ties the vision and strategy to the goals and objectives of the individuals and departments concerned.

- It breaks down the strategic plan into objectives and initiatives that have a direct relevance to the day-to-day activities of personnel.

- It ensures that the right data is gathered and input is provided for effective measurement of objectives.

- If an objective is not attained, it facilitates a clear understanding of why and helps identification of initiatives to achieve performance.

- It acts as an effective basis for resource allocation which focuses on both managing current performance as well as long-term value.

Simple as it may sound, it is important that we take care of certain important aspects while implementing the Balanced Scorecard. The Balanced Scorecard *is not*:

- a set of Key Performance Indicators (KPIs) as sometimes perceived by the leadership. It is a set of carefully chosen measures which drive strategic performance.

- a set of measures representing all the stakeholders. It represents the relationship between the various stakeholders in the light of current strategy.

- a KRA program. The objective of constructing a Balanced Scorecard is not to create a framework of management control, but to enable strategic decision making.

- a one-time event, but a continuum. Do not construct a Balanced Scorecard and let it sit. To be effective, it has to become a part of daily decision making.

- a measure of what can be measured conveniently. It should measure what needs to be measured to highlight aspects of performance important for decision making.

To be effective, the Balanced Scorecard needs to be systematically communicated across the organization. Care should be taken to ensure that everyone understands the Balanced Scorecard and uses it to manage the business.

SHIFTING FROM A BUDGET MANAGEMENT SYSTEM TO A STRATEGIC MANAGEMENT SYSTEM

We established from discussions in the previous sections that strategy development and deployment is critical to the way an organization creates and manages its performance measurements and performance management systems. As opposed to focusing only on financial measurements, which causes the organization to focus solely on the short term and budgets, creating a Balanced Scorecard of measurements, based upon the overall strategy, strategy maps, and strategic objectives should be the goal for any organization to better its chances for long-term success and sustainability.

Many organizations are focused on delivering shareholder value through budget managed systems. Typically, the steps followed to get there would comprise the following:

1. Define the purpose and aspirations of the organization

2. Understand competitive and environmental factors

3. Define organization strategy/operating plans

4. Establish annual goals/targets

5. Complete budget/resource allocation

6. Develop functional/departmental goals/targets

7. Assign individual KRA/budgets

8. Implement/manage daily performance

9. Review progress/performance

However, evidence suggests that the application of such a framework has not yielded the desired results. Interestingly, it is not strategy formulation which is under scrutiny, but *strategy implementation* or deployment that needs attention. Worldwide, research reveals astonishing facts that cut through the hype that surrounds the current frameworks of strategy implementation or deployment. The Baldrige criteria devotes an entire section (Item 2.1) to the discussion and understanding of how strategies are deployed throughout the organization.[13]

Statistical data, presented at the beginning of this chapter, discuss and demonstrate the importance of a well-developed, well-rounded (balanced), and well-deployed strategy and the overall impact it has on any organization. Therefore, as discussed previously, it is not only logical but imperative that an organization urgently create a framework to manage strategic-driven performance in order to achieve operational excellence. Hence, the strategic management system is a necessity and paradigm shift for organizations. This does not mean an organization gets rid of its budgets and financial tracking and reporting mechanism, rather it creates a measurement and management system that is based on a balanced set of metrics— not just financial—that are derived from its strategy. This point is further reinforced in Figure 6.19, with the message being the need to focus on strategic reviews as opposed to operational reviews. It is not the opinion of the authors that a budget management system is incorrect or will not work. Many organizations have used this approach successfully. However, employing a strategic management system helps align an organization around all the factors that are important to its well-being and success.

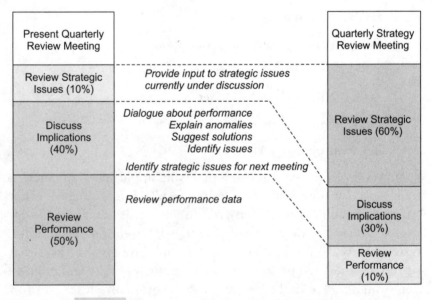

Fig. 6.19 The Operational Review to Strategic Review

SUMMARY

In order to help guarantee the sustainability and future success of any organization, a new paradigm shift requires it to focus on both financial and non-financial measures linked to the strategy of that organization. The Malcolm Baldrige National Quality Award criteria, which helps define a system of operational excellence, asks the organization to assess its ability to develop and deploy strategies, action plans, strategic objectives, goals, and targets.[14] The Balanced Scorecard approach, developed by Robert Kaplan and David P. Norton in the early 1990s, provides a recipe for organizations to follow that creates a balanced set of financial and non-financial measures that are based upon the organization's strategy.[15] The concept of developing a Balanced Scorecard allows an organization to move from a budget management system, one of focusing solely on short-term financial and operational performance, to a strategic management system, which aligns an organization's action plans and resources around achievement of organizational strategies, strategic objectives, and targets. In the past, budget management systems have worked successfully for many organizations, but by employing a strategic management system, an organization has total alignment, agreement, and support around all the factors that are important to its well-being and success, and that help deliver value to its customers.

REFERENCES

(1) Robert S. Kaplan and David P. Norton, "Translating Strategy into Action—The Balanced Scorecard," Harvard Business School Press, Boston, Massachusetts, USA, 1996.

(2) Ibid.

(3) Ibid.

(4) William A. Schiemann and John H. Lingle, "Bulls Eye: Hitting Your Strategic Targets Through High Impact Measurement," The Free Press, 1230 Avenue of the Americas, New York, NY, USA 10020, 1999.

(5) "SAP—Strategic Enterprise Management—Turning strategy into action; The Balanced Scorecard; David Norton, The Balanced Scorecard Collaborative, Inc., and by SEM Product Management, SAP AG, Neurostrasse 16.69190 Walldorf, Germany, May 1999.

(6) Robert S. Kaplan and David P. Norton, "Translating Strategy into Action—The Balanced Scorecard," Harvard Business School Press, Boston, Massachusetts, USA, 1996.

(7) "A Balanced Scorecard for Small Business"

C.W. Von Bergen
Southeastern Oklahoma State University, Management and Marketing Department Durant, Oklahoma, 74701-0609, USA, Phone: 580-745-2430; Fax: 580-745-7485; e-mail: cvonbergen@sosu.edu

Daniel C. Benco
Southeastern Oklahoma State University, Department of Accounting and Finance, Durant, Oklahoma 74701-0609, USA. Phone: 580-745-2498; Fax: 580-745-7485; e-mail: dbenco@sosu.edu

(8) "Balanced Scorecard—Implementation" in SME's—reflection in Literature and Practice-2GC Conference Paper, Henrick Andersen, Ian Cobbold and Gavin Lawrie, presented at SME Conference, Copenhagen, Denmark, 1991.

(9) Robert S. Kaplan and David P. Norton, "Translating Strategy into Action—The Balanced Scorecard," Harvard Business School Press, Boston, Massachusetts, USA, 1996.

(10) Malcolm Baldrige National Quality Award, United States Department of Commerce, United States Department of Commerce, Technology Administration, National Institute of Standards and Technology, Baldrige National Quality Award Program, Administration Building, Room A635, 100 Bureau Drive, Stop 1020, Gaithersburg, Maryland 20899-1020, USA. http://www.nist.gov/

(11) Ibid.

(12) Ibid.

(13) Ibid.

(14) Ibid.

(15) Robert S. Kaplan and David P. Norton, "Translating Strategy into Action—The Balanced Scorecard," Harvard Business School Press, Boston, Massachusetts, USA, 1996.

CHAPTER SEVEN

PLANNING FOR CUSTOMER-DRIVEN TRANSFORMATION

As we begin to think of the next steps relative to transforming the organization into being more customer centric, let us step back and think through the things we have done so far, do a recap that will help us lay the track for the succeeding chapters.

- In Chapter 1 (Developing a Customer-Focused Culture), we discussed what it meant to be customer focused and how an organization would behave if a customer-centric environment were in place. The lessons taught in Chapter 1 are to position the organization to promote a customer-focused culture and start aligning the organization to deliver on customer requirements, both stated and implied.

- Chapter 2 (Leveraging Strategies for Creating Stakeholder Value) introduced the concept of Economic Value-Added (EVA) and how EVA lays the foundation for the organization to embrace the concept of financial and non-financial measures resulting in a balanced set of measurements that are tied to the strategies of the organization.

- Chapters 3 and 4 (Assessing Organizational Capabilities) discuss a few models that can be used to assess the holistic health of the organization and identify strategic gaps. The Malcolm Baldrige National Quality Award (Baldrige) Performance Excellence model, European Foundation Quality Management (EFQM), and Software Engineering Institute Capability Maturity Model (SEI CMM) were explored in detail, each with a strong focus on assessing the strength of an organization's customer focus as well as the breadth and alignment of its process management system.

- The focus of Chapter 5 (Preparing the Organization for Change) was to discuss some basic elements required for change within the organization, dynamics associated with change, and how to prepare for and reinforce change throughout the organization. After all, business environments are dynamic and constantly changing. And to transform the organization's culture to one that is more customer focused, a formal change management system is required.

- Once customer requirements were understood and deployed to the organization, and the organization determined strategic performance gaps and developed strategies to address these, it now needs to align the organization to support this transformation. The purpose of Chapter 6 (Aligning the Organization for Transformation), therefore, was to create a balanced set of financial and non-financial metrics that are aligned with customer requirements and key organizational processes and support achievement of the organization's strategies. The concept of a Balanced Scorecard was introduced as a key performance tool in Chapter 6.

The linkages and the interactions between these chapters—and the ones to follow—are depicted in Figure 7.1. These linkages and interactions form the basis for a model to implement strategic change and subsequent tools for transforming the organization. As shown in Figure 7.1, the inputs for Chapter 7, for now, are the outputs of Chapters 3 and 4 (strategic gaps) and Chapter 6 (balanced set of metrics).

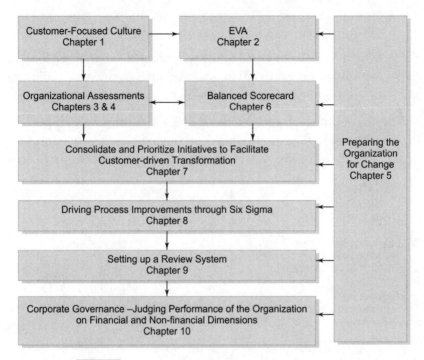

Fig. 7.1 Model for Implementing Strategic Change

CONSOLIDATING IMPROVEMENT OPPORTUNITIES AND IDENTIFYING INITIATIVES/PROCESSES

Since the inherent strength of an organization lies in its systems and processes that drive the multitude of actions contributing toward creating stakeholder value, it follows that an organization aspiring to compete and achieve business excellence, and address the constant climate of change, has to focus on identifying opportunities to strengthen its underlying systems and processes.

Organizational Assessments (Output of Chapters 3 and 4)

Chapters 3 and 4 discuss the use of the Baldrige and other assessment models that, by answering the following questions, identify the opportunities for improvement:

- Which approaches (systems/processes) need to be strengthened to achieve business excellence and poise the organization for change?

- In which areas does deployment (use and coverage) need to be strengthened to achieve consistent results?

- Which approaches or deployment areas need a closer look to improve their appropriateness and effectiveness in achieving desired outcomes (e.g., results)?

The organizational assessment findings can then be mapped, or used as inputs, to the organization's strategic objectives (Chapter 6), as illustrated in Figure 7.2. Once the mapping is complete, it is

	Number of Gaps from Organizational Diagonostics	F1	F2	F3	C1	C2	C3	B1	B2	B3	L1	L2	L3	L4
1	Complete deployment of 360 degree feedback to improve Leadership effectiveness							x						
2	Review Market Segmentation and respective Requirement definition	x			x									
3	Complete Deployment of Service Standards to all Regions		x			x								
4	Complete Collection of Comparative data in support of Strategic Objectives								x					
5	Identify Formal process and work systems to manage team based efforts										x			
6	Complete identification of Training needs and management of Training Calender/plans											x		
7	Deployment of policies to manage employee health safety and ergonomics												x	
8	Complete deployment of New Product Introduction process across all product lines						x							
9	Define and deploy HR plans linkage to Business Plans													x
10	Work on improvising the Strategic Planning process to be best in class									x				

Fig. 7.2 Map of Gaps from the Organizational Assessment to Strategic Objectives

necessary to think of the initiatives or high-level action plans that need to be launched in the organization to fix the gaps.

Identification of Key Initiatives to Address Strategic Measures (Output of Chapter 6)

In Chapter 6, we arrived at a set of measures linked to the strategies of the organization. In order to achieve the targets determined against the strategic objectives, the organization had to undertake a set of strategic initiatives. For each of the strategic objectives and their corresponding measures, a set of initiatives was selected and an initiative map prepared. The map highlighted the relationship between the strategic objectives and the initiatives (Figure 7.3). These initiatives were of two types:

1. Initiatives to improve the influence of the organization, such as entering new markets, acquiring companies, and so forth

2. Initiatives to strengthen the systems/processes of the organization, such as the new product development process

It is now time to reconcile between the two sets of initiatives, consolidate, and, perhaps, arrive at a larger set that is more comprehensive. When we talk of initiatives linked to the strategy of an organization, it appears to have limitations in that the organization oftentimes does not look beyond its own boundaries or does not look at other organizations for relative comparison or learnings. This limitation can be overcome through the use of the Baldrige and other models that challenge and stretch the organization.

Therefore, the larger set of initiatives are the ones that are key to the success of the organization and, hence, there is a need to align and prioritize them. This has been discussed in the following sections.

Initiatives and Processes

There are subtle differences between an initiative and a process. Generally speaking, processes enable an organization to achieve initiatives. For example, "launch the new quote-to-cash project" may be an initiative while the processes to enable this initiative could be:

Sr.	Strategic Initiative	F1	F2	F3	C1	C2	C3	C4	B1	B2	B3	B4	B5	L1	L2	L3	L4	Resp.
I1	Prepare and implement plans for acquiring the competitor plant at New Delhi	X	X	X	X	X	X	X		X	X	X	X					KK
I2	Prepare and implement plans to right size operations at Karnataka	X		X							X	X	X					PLJ
I3	Deploy a structured new product introduction process Prioritize development efforts	X	X				X	X			X							GH
I4	Prepare and implement plans to exit paper making by June XX	X		X									X					JKK
I5	Deploy a "Customer Relationship Management" system including web-based Customer Site				X	X	X	X	X	X								KL
I6	Review and re-design the internal processes which support customer/market contact processes				X	X		X	X	X		X	X					KK
I7	Design and implement a company wide cost reduction program	X		X									X					OLP
I8	Deploy a structured Performance Management System for all officers	X	X	X				X					X	X	X	X		FGH
I9	Develop an IT strategy in line with the company strategy till year XX		X	X						X			X				X	JUH

Fig. 7.3 Initiative Map Demonstrating the Relationship between Strategic Objectives and Initiatives

- Streamline the bids and proposals process

- Reduce order to install cycle time

- Deploy Oracle (the tool used for this project) in all regions by the end of the year

It may be useful, therefore, to generate a table such as Figure 7.4 that lists and aligns key initiatives and the corresponding processes.

Initiative	Processes
Open new markets in APAC	Streamline the Sales Channel Process
Increase supply chain effectiveness through outsourcing to external manufacturing	Complete Supplier Evaluation, Finalize Approved Vendor List
Achieve BIC inventory turns-10 or more in year XX	Improve Forecasting Process
Achieve margin improvement of 30 % or more	Complete Target Costing Model and Deploy across the Supply Chain

Fig. 7.4 Alignment of Initiatives with Processes

ALIGNMENT OF CUSTOMER REQUIREMENTS WITH AN ORGANIZATION'S PROCESSES

In Chapter 1, we positioned the customer as central and key to the success of the organization, and the reason why organizations exist. It is, therefore, imperative that the designs of processes are strongly linked to the needs and requirements of customers. In the 2004 Baldrige criteria,[1] the entire Category 6 is devoted to process management (refer to Chapter 3), and in particular Item 6.1 is on "value creation processes." The criteria ask, "How does the organization identify and manage its key processes to create *customer value* and achieve business success and growth?" Item 6.2 asks, "How does the organization manage its key processes that support the value creation processes?"

Organizations often forget to align the needs and expectations of the customers with the internal processes that fulfill those needs. Customers can usually identify exactly where performance needs to be improved. Many initiatives such as Six Sigma state that an organization's approach to project and process improvements should begin and end with the customer. The unfortunate reality of most implementation approaches is that customer expectations and needs quickly get lost in the attempt to improve processes.

As will be explained in Chapter 8, process improvement projects are usually selected based upon potential cost savings, an admirable goal. General Electric is a leader in implementing Six Sigma, and Jack Welch, in the book *Jack Welch and the GE Way* cites numerous examples of how GE improved its bottom-line financial results as a consequence of Six Sigma improvement projects.[2] However, discussions on improvements in customer satisfaction, customer loyalty, or customer retention are less common. The book also talks about how, early into its improvement efforts, customers were asking GE how Six Sigma improvement benefited them. Customers were not necessarily asking for cost savings to be passed on to them, although this was probably one unarticulated motivating factor. The customers were asking why process improvements saved GE money, but did little to simplify the way customers did business with GE. Many of the Six Sigma changes were completely invisible to the customer. The lesson here is that an organization's approach to process improvement should consider and show benefit to customers and shareholders alike.

Rick Schleuesner, master consultant for the Six Sigma Academy in Scottsdale, Arizona, states that the driving needs for process improvement include some external factors such as competition, environmental changes, and changes in customer expectations.[3] Schleuesner says that the need to change is usually externally driven, but it requires a lot of internal effort, attention, and commitment to make the change happen. Like the other discussions throughout this book, the need to change is pervasive, driven by a number of (external) factors, and impacts many aspects of the organization, including process management and improvement.

Alignment of Customer Needs and Process Performance

As we said before, since organizations exist to serve customers, it is only natural to first understand the link between an organization's processes and customer requirements. In Chapter 1, we discussed how IBM Rochester used customer inputs or requirements and synthesized them to identify the customer attributes (see Figure 1.3—Customer View Model) and aligned all internal processes to map into those requirements (see Figure 1.4—Alignment of IBM Rochester customer view model attributes with key processes and key process measurements).

For instance, IBM Rochester previously focused quite heavily on the "manufacturing" process, but customers stated that they did not view IBM Rochester as having a "manufacturing" process but rather a fulfillment process. Customers stated that they placed an order for a product, and that the product was delivered. What happened in between was irrelevant to them unless it caused the product to be shipped defective or late. Therefore, IBM Rochester expanded its overall fulfillment process to include the ordering sub-process, the sub-process used to hand-off the order to the manufacturing process, and the delivery sub-process. When the organization can link customer needs, expectations, and requirements to its processes, the process can be redesigned to improve not only the financial performance of the organization, but customer satisfaction as well.

Since the customer is the ultimate judge of performance, the organization must clearly understand customer expectations. It is against the customer's expectations that process performance will eventually be evaluated. Therefore, the organization must align internal processes around the customer's needs and expectations. The remaining part of this chapter will present a couple of tools that are particularly helpful in accomplishing this alignment. These tools are customer expectations/process matrices and Quality Function Deployment (QFD).

Customer Expectations–Process Matrix

A Customer Expectations–Process Matrix uses a row and column format to match customer expectations and processes. All customer expectations are listed on one axis and the value creating processes are listed on the other axis. A sample matrix is presented in Figure 7.5. Because the use of this model gets extremely complicated if 50 or 60 attributes are evaluated at one time, normally each major grouping such as products, sales, or installation is the focus of a separate matrix.

Customer Expectations– Process Matrix

Product or Service Performance Metric

Value Creating Processes Customer Expectations	PS-1	PS-2	PS-3	PS-4	PS-5	PS-6	PS-7	PS-8
A-1	◯	☆						
A-2		◯				△		
A-3		△	◯			△		
A-4			◯				☆	
A-5		◯			◯			
A-6		☆			◯	☆		
A-7								
A-8	☆					△		☆

☆   STRONG RELATIONSHIP

◯   MEDIUM RELATIONSHIP

△   WEAK RELATIONSHIP

Fig. 7.5 Customer Expectations–Process Matrix

On the vertical axis of the matrix are the customer expectations. Each attribute is listed, one on each row. On the horizontal axis, the processes that create value are listed. There may be one or more for each process. Each performance metric has its own column. The strength of the relationship between each attribute and each product or service requirement is indicated by the use of a symbol. In this example, strong, medium, and weak relationships are depicted.

If a row, such as A-7, has no product or service requirement associated with it, the implication is that the organization is not paying attention to how this attribute is created. If A-7 is very important to the customer, it could have serious negative consequences.

If a column, such as PS-4, has no impact on any attribute, the need for the product or service requirement must be questioned. Perhaps there is a valid reason for the requirement, but it is unrelated to customer expectations.

By using a matrix, it is possible to examine the relationship between customer expectations and the internal product or service requirements necessary to meet the customer's expectations. Accordingly, the matrix can be a very good planning tool. However, the matrix can be expanded substantially through the use of Quality Function Deployment (QFD).

Quality Function Deployment

Quality Function Deployment (QFD) is a planning tool that translates customer needs and expectations into product and service requirements, performance metrics, areas of responsibility, and priorities for action. QFD is sometimes referred to as "the House of Quality".[4] The use of QFD enhances customer satisfaction and reduces cycle time for product and service deployment and delivery. In essence, the use of QFD forces an organization to become customer centered. For an organization focused on process improvement, the use of QFD will identify the areas of responsibility and performance metrics quite clearly.

In the simplest form, QFD is a technique that translates customer expectations into product and service requirements or features. The Customer Expectations–Process Matrix can be used as a starting point to match customer requirements with processes, identifying performance metrics, and expanding these inputs into a House of Quality (HOQ) format. The goal is to harmonize product and service features with customer expectations.

Figure 7.6 depicts a Quality Function Deployment model, which illustrates the House of Quality format. In a HOQ format, the original labels for the two axes are, "What is expected" and "How to achieve it." Often, these are simply truncated to "what" and "how." Perhaps, more accurately, the "what" can be described as "customer expectations," on the left side of the HOQ. There is a row for each customer expectation. The "how" can be described as "product and/or service requirements," on the top of the HOQ. There is a column for each dimension of process performance. Thus, a single process might have three or four related columns.

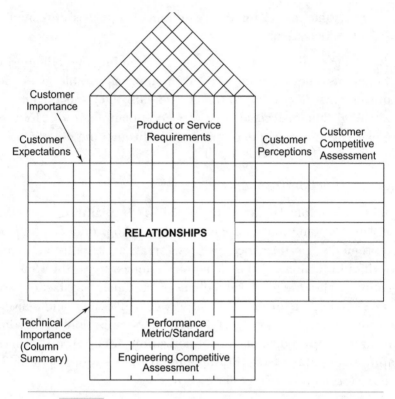

Fig. 7.6 Quality Function Deployment—House of Quality

To this basic HOQ, there are usually several additions. First, an organization will develop a performance metric or standard for each product or service requirement, at the bottom of the HOQ. For example, a standard could be to answer 90 percent of the phone calls on the first ring or to resolve all customer complaints within 24 hours. These are usually added to the bottom or the basement/ foundation of the HOQ so that each performance requirement, at the top of a column, has a corresponding performance metric or standard at the bottom of the same column. Obviously, the performance metric should correspond to what the customer expects.

Some organizations conduct their own competitive assessment on each of the performance requirements for key competitors. In this way, it identifies what it perceives to be its strengths and weaknesses. This internal self-assessment appears at the bottom (foundation) of the HOQ. As an example, with regard to most high technology products, the first products produced are often purchased by competitors, who disassemble the product using reverse engineering and identify the strengths and weaknesses of the product, design, and processes. The competitor builds the strength of the new innovation into its products, and avoids and/or exploits the weaknesses of the competing product. For personal computers and printers, an organization may spend a year of research and development to produce a new model. Within 60 days of introduction, all the new innovations are copied by competitors. When Motorola introduced a new pager, it took a Taiwanese company only weeks to come out with an equivalent product in the market.

The second addition to the HOQ are the actual customer perceptions. This addition is usually placed on the right side of the matrix so that each customer expectation row can be matched to a customer's perception of actual performance. This is where the feedback from customer satisfaction surveys, complaint data, customer focus groups, and customer interviews are fed into the QFD matrix. The customer perception column for example, consist of top box scores, top two scores, or mean values, for each corresponding question on a survey.

At this point, there are several considerations that are critical. The description of the customer expectations and customer perceptions should be in the customer's words. And the description of the customer perceptions should be harmonized with the relevant performance metric. That is, the wording of the customer expectation and the corresponding performance standard should be closely aligned with one another. This will make the customer perceptions, often gathered from customer satisfaction survey data, more actionable.

The feedback from customers can also be supplemented with a competitive assessment. By gathering competitive data, an organization can develop a profile that identifies strengths and weaknesses from the customer's perspective. Assessment tools discussed in Chapter 3 and Chapter 4 could be used. The competitive assessment should be compared to the results of the self-assessment (at the bottom of the HOQ) described earlier. This allows the validation of strengths and weaknesses, providing both an internal view as well as a customer's view. If there are major discrepancies between customer perceptions and actual performance, there could be important implications for marketing and communication strategies.

Another addition to the HOQ is the roof. The roof is simply a correlation matrix among the product and service requirements. The purpose of the correlation matrix is to show how the performance areas interact with one another. These are qualitative correlations assigned by experienced individuals. The correlations could be strongly positive, positive, negative, strongly negative, or none at all. For example, the horsepower of an automobile engine may be strongly positively correlated with acceleration (as measured by 0–60 miles per hour elapsed time), but strongly negatively correlated with fuel economy (miles per gallon) and negatively correlated with vehicle weight. The design specification involves a series of trade-offs among performance requirements that will optimize value to the customer. For example, a customer may want a fast automobile but also wants it to be large and roomy, thus adding weight, which compromises speed.

The HOQ is nearly complete. As discussed earlier, primary attention should be given to those areas that are important to customers. Therefore, there should be some kind of importance rating determined for each customer expectation. An "importance" column is, therefore, added on the left side of the HOQ in Figure 7.6. The most important customer expectations should receive priority attention, particularly if performance is low on these.

The importance of each product or service requirement should also be rated. This is done by multiplying the customer importance for each expectation by the strength of relationship. A strong relationship might be assigned a value of five, a moderate relationship a value of three, and a weak relationship a value of one. The importance weights could be calculated for each column to obtain an aggregate importance rating for each product and service requirement. This is indicated by the technical importance row at the bottom of the HOQ. Requirements that have a large impact on the customer, by influencing several expectations, should be of high interest to the organization.

There are some pragmatic limitations to the use of QFD. It is not at all unusual for customers to identify hundreds of attributes that may be used to evaluate a product or service. Of these, perhaps 30 to 40 may be relatively important to the customer. Developing a HOQ with 30 to 100 customer expectations, with one row for each expectation, would be a daunting task as there may be an equal number of performance requirements, with one column for each of these. Needless to say, a 50 by 50 matrix for the basic HOQ would be quite cumbersome. The solution is to decompose the total project into smaller segments. If the decomposition is done based on processes, a Six Sigma team will find the unit of analysis quite useful. For example, a sales process might be under review. Customer expectations of sales might be expressed as a salesperson's knowledge, consultative relationship, frequency of contact, follow-up, and friendliness, among others. A list of 10 customer expectations/attributes is quite workable in a HOQ.

Another approach to decomposing a larger set of customer requirements may occur when there are multiple types of customers, each with different expectations, requirements, and importance ratings. For instance, a new, inexperienced customer may have a different set of requirements and expectations than a long-term customer who is very experienced in the use of the product. For example, the quality of product documentation, may be very important to the new customer, but less important to the experienced customer.

A HOQ model could be developed at the process levels such as sales, billing, or customer service, so that the interrelationships among processes could be identified. For example, if an organization has seven key processes, seven other specific HOQs could be developed. The organization would find a HOQ model based on processes to be most beneficial in identifying and prioritizing improvement opportunities.

SELECTION AND PRIORITIZATION OF PROCESSES

Without detracting from the importance of Chapter 8, there are a variety of approaches that could be considered when selecting and prioritizing processes. A few of those approaches are presented in the following pages. One way could be to look at processes that are "customer impacting." These would, obviously, merit greater attention. For example, if the customers are not happy with new product introduction (e.g., new products are reaching them late), it is essential that there be a stronger focus on that process. In other words, in the priority listing that would qualify as number one. This is in line with our discussion in the earlier sections on how to establish alignment between a process and the customer.

The next category of processes that might require immediate attention would be those that are operationally important for the organization. For example, if the time interval between a quote and the actual realization of cash is too long, obviously this process needs to be dealt with immediately. In one company, when they realized that the "quote-to-cash" cycle time was far too long when compared to competition and way too long when compared to benchmarks, a whole project team was created with the express objective of reducing the time interval. Called the "Interval Reduction Project," disparate processes were all unified and integrated through a single SAP platform, as opposed to several legacy IT systems that contributed to the long cycle times.

The next category to look at could be those processes affecting the employees of the organization. For example, in a global setting, employee performance appraisal processes in an organization could be different in different countries. For the purposes of uniformity and consistency, it would be prudent to define and deploy a common process across the organization. An example in an organization was the use of what they called the Global Performance Platforms (GPP). Deployed globally, it resulted in a user friendly common process for performance reviews.

Therefore, in terms of a time-bound action plan, the above categorization may be mapped to some kind of codes depicting levels of priority. For example, a code of A may mean "customer impacting" that needs to be done immediately. B might mean "operationally important" that needs to be completed in not more than three months, and so on. Figure 7.7 gives a template on how to prioritize processes.

Another example of a method used by an organization is illustrated in Figure 7.8. In this example, the prioritization process is used to select a project as a Six Sigma opportunity. Figure 7.9

Process(es)	Category	End Date for Completion
New Product Introduction Process	Customer Impacting	A
Quote-to-Cash	Operational Importance	B
Warranty Reduction	Operational Importance	B
Global Reverse Supply Chain	Customer Impacting	A
Software Quality	Customer Impacting	A
Repair Process	Customer Impacting	A
Zero Latency–Bids and Proposals	Operational Importance	B
Inventory Reduction	Operational Importance	B
Gross Margin Realization	Operational Importance	B
Leadership Training	Employee Impacting	C
Performance Appraisal-Global Deployment	Employee Impacting	C
Early Supplier Involvement	Operational Importance	B
Outsourcing of Factories	Operational Importance	B

Code :

A—Immediate
B—Within three months
C—Within six months

Fig. 7.7 Prioritization of Processes

Project Prioritize, Select, Define Process

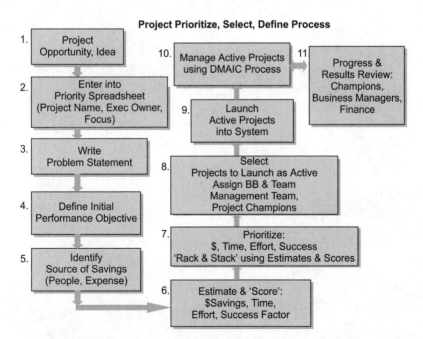

Fig. 7.8 Process Used for Prioritization in Six Sigma Projects

1	2	3	4	5	6	Selection Criteria (score as 9, 7, 3, 1: see Fig. 7.10 for score rules)				11
						7	8	8	9	
Project Name	Problem Statement	Focus (Customer, Process, Strategic Change, Waste)	Exec Owner Project Champion, Black Belt	Performance Objective (Defects, Process Performance—Be Specific, DPPM, OQL, Rolled Yield, Rework, Cycle time)	Source of $ Savings (People $, Capital $, Material $, Expense $) (list specific numbers & assumptions)	$ Savings (Hard) (annual)	Time (Duration)	Effort (# People & $, Expense $, Cap $)	Success Factor (1-Risk)	Total Score
										0
										0
										0
										0
										0
										0
										0
										0
										0
Example: Estimating bid submittal process	Estimating and Proposal generation takes too long and costs too much	Core Process	'Luigi' 'Robert' 'Debra'	Achieve cycle time < 14 days; reduce number of proposals handbacks to 3 or less, achieve < 1000 dppm submittal defects; reduce proposal generation cost to less than $ 10K/proposal.	10 Bid and Submittal Preparation	9 $ 1 Million	7 6 months	9 3 person team	No Cap, No IT, Multiple affected groups, moderate duration workgroups; small	32
										0
										0
										0

Fig. 7.9 Project Selection Worksheet

illustrates an example of a project selection worksheet, again used to prioritize actions and resources used for process improvement. Finally, Figure 7.10, depicts an example of a scoring matrix that is

Scoring Rules to Select/Prioritize Processes

Score	$ Savings (Hard) (Annual)	Time (Duration)	Effort (# People & $; Expense $, Cap $)	Success Factor (1-Risk)
9	> $250K (High)	< 4 mo. (Short)	< 3 (Small)	High No capital No IT No suppliers Small work group affected Short duration Small project team size
7	$100K-$250K (Moderate)	4-8 mo. (Moderate)	4-6 (Moderate)	Moderate No capital No IT Some suppliers Multiple work groups affected Moderate duration Small project team size
3	$50K-$100K (OK)	8-12 mo. (Long)	6-10 (Large)	OK Some capital Some IT Numerous suppliers Many work groups affected Long duration Moderate project team size
1	<$50K (Small)	> 12 mo. (Very long)	> 10 (Very large)	Low Significant capital Significant IT Very many suppliers Very many work groups affected Very long duration Large project team size

					Total Score
For example:					
Project A	9 $300K	7 7 months	3 8 person project team	3 OK: some cap, no IT, no suppliers, many work groups affected moderate duration, moderate project team	22
Project B	3 $75K	9 4 months	9 2 person team	9 no cap, no IT, no suppliers, small work group affected short duration, small project team size	30

Fig. 7.10 Scoring Matrix

used to quantify factors that help an organization decide what process should be improved. This is based upon assigned weightage to those items most important for selecting and prioritizing projects. For example, time, effort, and risk.

DETERMINING KEY PROCESS PERFORMANCE METRICS

Having prioritized which set of processes an organization needs to focus on, it would be useful to now think of using tools such as Six Sigma to drive process improvement. When we talk of process improvements, no matter which tool we use, it is necessary to think of the corresponding measures to determine the effectiveness of the processes we are trying to improve. We can, perhaps, generate a matrix such as Figure 7.11 that establishes linkage between processes and measures.

Processes	Measures	Goals or Targets
Reduce cycle time from order receipt to install	Cycle time	50 %
Complete deployment of new product introduction process for all products by end of fiscal year XX	% of new products that met the General Availability (GA) date	50 %
Complete core competency training across the organization	Number of associates covered in fiscal year XX	75%

Fig. 7.11 Linkage of Processes and Measures

SUMMARY

Organizations exist to serve customers. Organizations run by processes. Processes need to be aligned with what is important to customers and support not only an internal view, but an external one as well. There are a number of methods that can be used to translate customer requirements into process requirements. For example, Customers Expectation–Process Matrix or a Quality Function Deployment (QFD) model. The important aspect is to first align processes with customer requirements and identify which processes support meeting customer expectations and why, and then work on prioritizing those identified processes. The bottom line is preparing the organization for customer-driven transformation. This is just one of several factors that invoke change in the organization albeit the most important one.

REFERENCES

(1) Malcolm Baldrige National Quality Award, United States Department of Commerce, United States Department of Commerce, Technology Administration, National Institute of Standards and Technology, Baldrige National Quality Award Program, Administration Building, Room A635, 100 Bureau Drive, Stop 1020, Gaithersburg, Maryland 20899-1020, USA. http://www.nist.gov.

(2) "Jack Welch and the GE Way," by Robert Slater, McGraw-Hill Publishing Company, 11 West 19th Street, New York, New York, USA 10011, 1999.

(3) "Take the Mystery out of Process Improvement," Quality Magazine, 1050 IL Route, Suite 200, Bensenville, Illinois, 60106, USA December 2002.

(4) "Customer Centered Six Sigma: Linking Customers, Process Improvement, and Financial Results," ASQ Quality Press, Milwaukee, Wisconsin, USA, 2001, by Earl Naumann and Steven H. Hoisington.

CHAPTER EIGHT

IMPLEMENTING PROCESS IMPROVEMENT

There are a number of methods that can be used to define and document processes, some of which have been discussed in the previous chapters of this book. The basic definition of a process, however, is an activity performed to achieve a desired result. The three basic steps of a process are input, activity, and output. Chapter 7 discussed in detail the creation of processes and emphasized the need to factor customer requirements into the input, activity, and output portions of all processes. Chapter 3 discussed the use of the Baldrige model for business assessment and, ultimately, improvement of the organization. Process management is a major element of the Baldrige criteria (Category 6),[1] and essentially asks one to describe the key processes used to manage the organization, how customer requirements are incorporated into the process, how the process is measured and managed to ensure that operational performance requirements are being met, and what in-process measurements are in place to ensure that the process is performing as expected and will continue to perform in control. This chapter will explore a couple of methods used to assess and improve process performance, namely Six Sigma and Rummler-Brache. Worldwide, both are accepted as major methods for improving process performance. Before delving into these methods, it is important to discuss the need to identify the processes that warrant improving.

SELECTING PROCESSES FOR IMPROVEMENT

Selecting the "right" processes that need to be improved is as critically important as the method used to improve the process itself. In an organization that has an on-going continuous improvement effort, the selection of a process is less critical. Regardless of whether the selection of a process to be improved is for the first time or for the fiftieth time, there are some issues that the organization must consider. The four primary issues to consider are the relevance of the processes to the organization's strategic goals, the costs associated with a particular process, the importance of the process output to the customer, and the competitive strengths and weaknesses of the organization. Before discussing these issues in detail, let us discuss the processes that should NOT be selected.

Which Process NOT to Select for Improvement

There are several situations that will undermine or constrain the effectiveness of continuous process improvement efforts. These are red flags that should be avoided or corrected before starting on a project to improve a process. There are four situations that would cause the improvement effort to be ineffective.

1. Lack of Senior Management Support and/or Commitment

Process improvement efforts should not be started if there is no clear support from the senior management for the improvement effort. The reason for this is that a majority of an organization's key processes cut across organizational and functional boundaries. In most organizations, senior management involvement and support is necessary to ensure the participation of all the relevant parties. In essence, the senior management becomes a coordinating mechanism that breaks down barriers associated with cross-organization, cross-functional process improvement efforts.

Process improvement, regardless of the method used, will require resources. If done correctly, process owners, users, and customers (internal or external customers) should be involved in the activity of defining process steps and expected levels of performance. This is especially true of the Rummler-Brache methodology discussed later in this chapter. Team members may be widely dispersed geographically, so the organization may incur travel expenses. Since the budget is controlled by the senior management, resource allocation requires their approval and support.

2. No Support from Process Owners

Related to the issue of lack of support from the senior management is the issue of lack of support from process owners. For instance, a human resources vice-president may not be particularly excited about an effort devoted to employee training and development. Without the vice-president's support, implementing changes would be difficult.

Since most organizations are structured around departments or functional areas, the department head may play the role of a process owner. A process may depend heavily on the information technology (IT) department. If an IT manager is unwilling to change procedures or modify databases, significant process changes are unlikely. Thus, functional area managers who are centrally involved in a specific process should be involved with the process improvement efforts. There can be many sub-owners of a process due to its cross-functionality and/or complexity.

Finally, a process owner, regardless of functional responsibility or reporting structure, may not cooperate with a team wanting to improve its process. After all, this may imply a level of incompetence on the part of the process owner, whose job it has been to ensure the efficient performance of the process.

3. Ambiguous Processes

Some processes are ambiguous and ill-defined. Ambiguity may include the lack of a clearly defined starting or ending point, lack of identification of specific customer inputs or process outputs, or lack of clearly defined process steps. Process ambiguity results in a vague definition of process performance or control metrics and measurements. Without understanding process performance parameters, including costs and cycle times, a team's efforts would be wasted on trying to improve the process. The best place for the team to start would be to define the "As-Is" state of the process, the concept discussed in Chapter 7.

4. Trivial Processes

When processes are selected, particularly for the initial project, they should be significant and important areas, not minor or trivial. Since initial projects are evaluated very critically, there should be some significant benefits that can be documented. The more significant processes have higher costs, more employees, longer cycle times, and a more direct impact on the customers. When benefits are achieved in these processes, other employees in the organization are quick to recognize the value. Benefits can also be tied to significant financial performance improvements. However, if a process is of no significance, others in the organization may be skeptical of the value from the proposed improvement efforts.

Selecting the Right Processes for Improvement

There are four characteristics that should be considered when selecting the right process for improvement. The process should be strategically important to an organization's overall goals. The process should have significant costs—either labor or material—associated with it. Often, processes with high cycle times also have significant costs. The process should also be important to customers, and it should build upon competitive strengths or correct weaknesses. Each of these four characteristics is explained below.

1. Strategic Importance

Virtually all organizations develop annual strategic goals and plans that address areas such as revenue growth, cost reduction, customer satisfaction, and/or new product development initiatives. Some organizations have strategic goals that address the development and retention of employees. Others have strategic goals that address alliances or partnerships with other organizations in the value chain.

Yet others, like Johnson Controls, Inc., have strategic goals for continuous process improvement through the identification of key processes and initiatives of the organization.

The senior management is likely to be supportive of initiatives that directly support strategic goals. Often, this results in resource allocation to the process improvement efforts. Others in the organization will also be more willing to support or be involved in process improvement because of its linkage to strategic goals and the high visibility it will ultimately receive. For most organizations, the strategic goals are also related to the other issues of cost, importance to the customer, and competitive position.

2. Costs

High-cost processes are good candidates for process improvement. The logic behind this is simple. If a 20 percent cost reduction is achieved in a process that consumes $500,000 in resources, the savings to the organization are $100,000. If a 20 percent cost reduction is achieved in a process that consumes $200,000, the savings are only $50,000. For most process improvement projects, the time and effort required by an improvement team are the same for a $100,000 savings project as they are for a $50,000 savings project.

The processes that are strategically important and consume high costs are usually also important to the customer. Rather than the internal focus within an organization, the next issues to consider while selecting processes are external. These are customers and competitors.

3. Importance to Customers

Processes that are important to customers are prime candidates for improvement. An organization needs to examine processes that constitute the key drivers of customer satisfaction or dissatisfaction. One of the predominant lessons to be learned from this book is the importance of listening and learning from customers and applying what they say to the organization's continuous improvement efforts. That is, an organization should focus its improvement efforts on processes that have the highest impact on customer satisfaction or dissatisfaction, as opposed to only using costs or cycle time.

It is also important to observe processes from the customer's point of view. IBM Rochester focused on a number of processes that were felt to be important, including the manufacturing process. As discussed in Chapter 7, customers stated, however, that they did not view the manufacturing process as very important, but only cared about the fact that the product was easy to order and delivered as they expected. This caused IBM Rochester to focus on the larger fulfillment process, which included the ordering sub-process, the sub-process of handing the order to manufacturing, and the delivery and installation sub-processes. Customers stated that they were only concerned with the fact that they could order a product, and IBM delivered it.[2]

4. Builds on Competitive Strengths or Weaknesses

An organization can determine its competitive strengths or weakness by making performance comparisons against its competitors. In this way, a competitive strength could be exploited or a weakness improved. Comparing an organization to its competitors can be done in a number of ways such as gathering information through the organization's own customers, especially if customers deal with several competing organizations for the same products and services. Customers are continually making competitive comparisons when selecting suppliers.

There is a danger in comparing an organization's performance to the industry average. While an average is an easy reference point, it is just what the name implies, an average. Some organizations will be above average and some below. It is rare for an organization's strategic goal to become an industry average. Most organizations have goals to gain market share and revenue, which is accomplished by trying to be the best, or one of the best, in their respective industry. Therefore, it is often helpful to identify scores against an individual competitor. When a customer leaves an organization, the customer usually goes to the industry leader, not an industry laggard, or the industry average.

Having explored the concept of which process to select—or not select—for process improvement, let us now discuss two major process improvement methodologies. These process improvement methodologies are Six Sigma and Rummler-Brache. Both are accepted worldwide, but Six Sigma has gained more popularity in recent years.

PROCESS IMPROVEMENTS THROUGH SIX SIGMA

The concept of Six Sigma is emerging as a universally accepted practice of identifying breakthrough thinking to fundamentally and significantly improve an organization's performance. Its basic premise is around the use of data and processes to define change.

What Is Six Sigma?

Six Sigma has enjoyed success in global companies for over 15 years. Pioneered by Motorola in the 1980s, but boosted by the efforts of General Electric (GE) and others in the late 1990s, Six Sigma is a business strategy to help an organization become better, faster, and lower its cost by focusing on breakthrough improvements to key processes, services, and products. In its simplest definition, Six Sigma is a strategic initiative to eliminate waste and mistake proof the processes that create value for customers. A Six Sigma culture strives for the continuous improvement of an organization's processes, services, and products and is more about managerial innovation than about statistical process control.[3]

Six Sigma results in the development of a uniform way to measure and monitor organizational performance and sets extremely high expectations and improvement goals. The measuring and monitoring of performance deals with a variety of statistical applications, but all of the statistical analysis aims at managing and reducing variation and waste in productive processes. Sigma is a statistical unit of measure which reflects variation in a process, service, or product. The sigma scale reflects measurements such as defects per unit, defects per process step, parts per million, and the probability of a failure or error. A Six Sigma level of performance means that there will be only 3.4 defects or less per million opportunities for error (see Figure 8.1). This is a near-perfect level of performance. In its purest application, an organization will apply Six Sigma tools to solid process or project management skills to improve the performance of a process through elimination of waste—such as non-value added

Six Sigma is a Measure of Variation		
	Defects per million of opportunities	Percentage Defects
Two Sigma	308,000	30.1%
Three Sigma	66,807	6.7%
Four Sigma	6.210	0.62%
Five Sigma	233	0.0233%
Six Sigma	3.4	0.0000034%

Fig. 8.1 Defect Opportunities and Percent Defect per Six Sigma Level of Performance

steps, and defects. Performance levels improve with higher sigma levels. Defect levels are counted and compared against opportunities for error within the process. Determining what constitutes an opportunity for error should always be defined from the customer's perspective. For instance, an organization could count the number of defects found within a product it assembles and compare this with the total number of parts contained in the product. However, customers are not concerned about the number of parts within the product that are good or bad, they will only care about the final product—whether it is good or bad. The ultimate goal may not be to reduce defect levels to a statistical Six Sigma level of performance, but rather, significantly improve performance of the process from its previous level.

Opportunities for improvement are identified throughout the organization in a number of ways including feedback from customers, employees, and partners—any major stakeholder. Organizations should look at areas that are causing the greatest amount of pain and inefficiency. Examples might be a high level of complaints by customers; cost over-runs; excessive overtime; or an unusually high level of outstanding, unpaid claims. Resources, sometimes referred to as Black Belts, are formally trained on a plethora of statistical tools and techniques and the overall Six Sigma methodology. Black Belts employ project management skills utilizing a five-step model—define, measure, analyze, improve, and control process (DMAIC) (see Figure 8.2). Using statistical tools and techniques, they work with a project team and data that are generated from the process or procedure to determine optimal performance

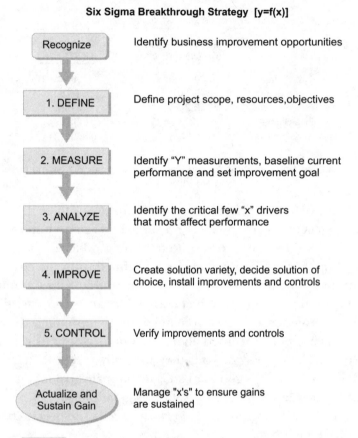

Six Sigma Breakthrough Strategy [y=f(x)]

Recognize — Identify business improvement opportunities

1. DEFINE — Define project scope, resources, objectives

2. MEASURE — Identify "Y" measurements, baseline current performance and set improvement goal

3. ANALYZE — Identify the critical few "x" drivers that most affect performance

4. IMPROVE — Create solution variety, decide solution of choice, install improvements and controls

5. CONTROL — Verify improvements and controls

Actualize and Sustain Gain — Manage "x's" to ensure gains are sustained

Fig. 8.2 Six Sigma 5-Step Breakthrough Strategy Process

levels and solutions to eliminate waste and improve operational efficiency. Project team members are individuals from the organization who are involved in the targeted process on a regular basis.

Often, we use percentages to assess organizational performance. This is a natural tendency and we sometimes find ourselves expressing events in terms of probability such as: "There is a 50–50 chance of this event occurring." One would probably view a process operating properly 99 percent of the time as good. But what does this mean in a practical application? Ninety-nine percent performance means:

- 20,000 lost articles of mail per hour
- 5,000 incorrect surgical operations per week

- 200,000 wrong drug prescriptions each year week in the United States
- No electricity for almost seven hours each month
- Unsafe drinking water for almost one hour each month

Could you afford to tolerate this level of performance from your organization? When put in this perspective, 99 percent performance does not sound all that good. How about a 10-fold improvement to 99.9 percent? This sounds pretty good, until it is put into perspective. A 99.9 percent performance means:

- Two short or long landings daily at most major airports
- 32,000 checks deducted from the wrong banking account per hour
- 54,000 lost articles of mail per week
- No phone service for nearly 27 minutes each month
- 1.7 errors per day in hospital Intensive Care Units (ICUs), of which one in five is a fatal error.[4]

Many performance levels have been defined by customers. What appears to be an acceptable level of performance to an organization may, in fact, be unacceptable from the customer's point of view. There is rarely any controversy about the adequacy of a process or product that is achieving a Six Sigma level of performance.

A Mistake Costs How Much?

A more revealing insight into levels of performance using Six Sigma is the use of costs associated with better levels of performance. For example, a process operating at plus or minus a Four Sigma level of performance will generate 6,210 defects per million opportunities. Examples of defects in this case could be defective parts or an incorrect answer to a question. If it is estimated that each defect costs $1,000 to correct, the cost to an organization is $6,210,000. At plus or minus Five Sigma, the level of defects drops to 233, and the total cost of the defects then declines to $233,000, a savings of nearly $6 million. At the near-perfect level of plus or minus Six Sigma, defects are almost eliminated, constituting only 3.4 defects per million opportunities, and reducing the cost of defects to only $3,400.

Johnson Controls, Inc., began its Six Sigma journey in early 2000 and by the end of 2001 had achieved nearly $100 million in cost savings from process improvement projects. In addition, at locations around the world, Six Sigma produced more than a 30 percent improvement in warranty costs, customer returns, and areas relative to inventory management. Six Sigma also contributed to nearly a six percentage point improvement in customer satisfaction due to improvements in product reliability and customer processes such as ordering and billing.[5]

Six Sigma is more than just cost savings as it also frees up personnel capacity. This allows an organization to do more with its existing staff (e.g., add services, increase sales, write more software codes, etc.). Six Sigma also improves customer (stakeholder) satisfaction. This can result in benefits such as more referrals, higher employee and customer loyalty, and improved staff productivity.

What Makes Six Sigma Different?

There are numerous quality models and initiatives available to improve operations. Some of the more famous of these models include ISO 9000, Malcolm Baldrige National Quality Award assessments, standards, and regulations. Six Sigma provides a (proven) methodology that allows an organization to significantly improve process performance. The rigorous scrutiny of Six Sigma allows an organization to identify significant continuous improvement opportunities that are based on factual information and data as against gut feel instincts. The results can be staggering, and the manufacturing and service industries have already proven the value and intensity Six Sigma can add to an organization. The experiences at Johnson Controls, Inc., in implementing a Six Sigma culture, have demonstrated that the administrative, sales, and back office processes yield more than five times the improvement in waste and defects elimination than manufacturing or engineering processes.[6] This may be due to the fact that organizations have employed a number of methodologies over time to improve manufacturing and engineering processes that have resulted in significant improvements already. It may also emphasize the fact that administrative activities, duties, and processes are inherently ripe for wasted effort. For instance, significant waste exists with patient billing for services provided by different providers within a health care organization.

PROCESS IMPROVEMENTS THROUGH THE USE OF RUMMLER-BRACHE METHODOLOGY

The Rummler-Brache group's process improvement and management methodology was developed by Allen P. Brache and Geary A. Rummler in the mid-1990s to address performance problems and opportunities in organizations utilizing existing resources.[7] The methodology has been tried and proven by many organizations, including Motorola, General Motors, Ford Motor Company, and Johnson Controls, Inc. Its premise is based on improvement of a cross-functional business process because of a critical business issue. Rummler-Brache is a systematic methodology for analyzing current processes for performance improvement, and then re-documenting the process format. Rummler-Brache is dependent upon trained facilitators to help process teams define current process steps (As Is) and then describe changes to the process—or a totally new process—based upon delivering customer requirements.

Typically, the first step in the Rummler-Brache methodology is to form a team of the current process owners and users who can define how they feel a certain process is supposed to be performed. One of the key differentiators of this methodology from others is that it places a heavy emphasis on understanding customer requirements and mapping process steps to support these. One of its disadvantages is that it lacks a solid base to measure process performance and conformance to customer requirements.

Another distinguishing feature of this method is the use of "swim lanes" in which to place process steps. As opposed to a normal process map that one follows from the top of the page to the bottom, a Rummler-Brache process map is read from left to right and contains rows that correspond to functional organizations. In this way, process steps that are to be performed by a particular organization reside in that row or "swim lane" assigned to them. A process sub-owner or user of the process can look across the page at all the process steps that are their responsibility. This uniqueness also facilitates a swim lane owner to visibly see the supplier of the input to their process step as well as the customer of the process step that they perform. Figure 8.3 depicts a typical process flow diagram and Figure 8.4 depicts the same process flow diagram in Rummler-Brache format with the associated swim lanes.

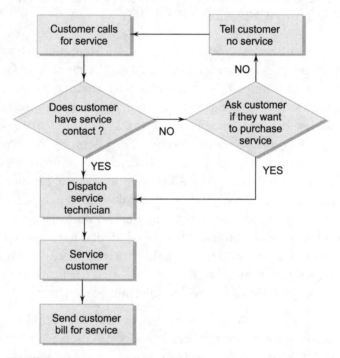

Fig. 8.3 Simple Flow Diagram for Customer Service Process

IMPERATIVE FOR DEVELOPING TRAINED FACILITATORS AND PROCESS IMPROVEMENT LEADERS

Continuous and effective improvement of any sort, regardless of whether it applies to a process or not, requires the use of a trained and talented group of individuals. This requires dedicated resources and some amount of investment. If properly managed by the organization, these individuals can easily reap the costs of their salaries, benefits, and training from a few major improvements within the organization. Organizations sometimes place more value and attention on hard, technical skills such as engineers or programmers, yet effective "project managers" can have the greatest

Swim Lanes

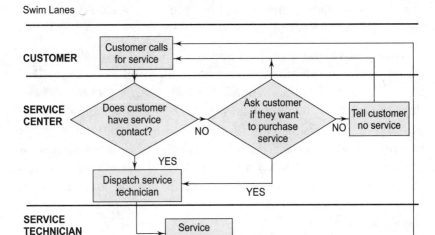

Fig. 8.4 Customer Service Process with Swim Lanes

impact on an organization. Engineers do not necessarily make the best project managers and vice versa. It is important that an organization does not shortchange itself on project management/ process management/problem solving skills. A balanced portfolio of skills is required for an organization to be most effective.

Six Sigma Black Belts, Champions, Green Belts

Six Sigma utilizes a cadre of specially trained resources to identify and improve processes. Black Belts lead teams through a five step process (define, measure, analyze, improve, and control—DMAIC) that establishes a baseline level of performance in which to base and compare process improvement after the changes have been identified and implemented. Because this methodology is based on the pervasive use of data—and data analysis through the use of advanced statistical techniques—training for Black Belts lasts about four weeks. Black Belts need to have good project management skills, should be able to work with others to get things done (Six Sigma improvement teams), and should be able to understand and apply advanced data analysis tools.

Champions manage projects and Black Belts. Their role is to help the organization identify improvement opportunities, assign Black Belts to the projects, and break down any barriers that the Black Belts encounter. Their focus should be on managing a large portfolio of projects through Black Belts assigned to them, ensuring that projects stay on track. Training required for Champions is about one week and should focus on a high level of project management and statistical techniques, on effectively managing individuals and projects, as well as on defining improvement opportunities and translating these into effective projects for Black Belts.

Some organizations use Green Belts to work on process improvements, sometimes in conjunction with Black Belts, sometimes on their own (for easier projects requiring less advanced statistical techniques), and sometimes as part of process improvement teams. At Johnson Controls, Inc., Green Belts are members of a Six Sigma team under the direction of a Black Belt. They receive their training from Black Belts, which may be one to two weeks in duration. Green Belts should possess analytical skills to a lesser degree than Black Belts, and also be trained in effective project management skills.

Rummler-Brache Facilitators

Rummler-Brache facilitators lead teams of individuals on defining and improving processes. They are trained on the Rummler-Brache methodology. This takes about one week. These facilitators need to have good facilitation skills, with an uncanny ability to get process teams to work together to define and improve processes in which they are intimately involved. A Rummler-Brache facilitator needs to have good process management skills, be a good communicator, and possess good people management and team building skills. They need to understand process mapping and how to gather customer requirement and translate these into process steps.

LEVERAGING INFORMATION TECHNOLOGY AND SYSTEMS TO STRENGTHEN PROCESSES

In the context of process definition and process improvement, the idea of strengthening processes through the use of information technology and systems has been left for the last. This is not to downplay its importance, but rather to emphasize the point that information technology (IT) and systems should be an outcome of process data needs. Too often, organizations attempt to define a process around an IT solution. This is counter productive to everything that has been described about processes and process management thus far. If done correctly, processes are defined based on their role in delivering customer requirements. Process measurements should define how the process is performing in delivering these requirements to customers or in meeting the performance expectations of the organization. The data needs supporting the process should drive the definition of an information technology or system solution. Sometimes, a process will have to be tweaked slightly to accommodate an "off-the-shelf" solution that comes close to meeting all the data needs supporting the process. But this should be minor in comparison to the rest of the function the IT solution provides. Once again, the process should drive the IT solution, and not vice versa.

Information technology and system solutions can help an organization effectively manage process performance. In many cases, they can automate process steps that were once done manually. If used effectively by process improvement teams, IT solutions can enhance the productivity of any process. The caution here again is to ensure that information technology does not drive the improvement. At Johnson Controls, Inc., Black Belts are taught that IT solutions are the last thing that can be proposed as part of a process improvement. All requests for IT changes or new system acquisitions are carefully scrutinized to ensure that all other possible avenues have been explored first. After all, IT solutions are quite expensive for an organization, and in some cases, licenses are required for each user, increasing costs further.

Information technology can be used quite effectively to monitor process performance and alert the organization if the process drifts out of control. IT systems can be used to store historical data on which to base comparison, or to create baseline levels of performance. And they can help automate manual steps of the process.

SUMMARY

There are many issues that must be considered when selecting process improvement efforts. The processes should be strategically important, have significant associated costs, be important to customers, and consider competitive performance. Unfortunately, most process improvements in the past have focused almost exclusively on cost and cycle time reduction. The use of competitive analysis can build on competitive strengths and/or correct weaknesses. By using a combination of these considerations, an organization can develop a balanced approach to selecting the "right" processes. Once the "right" process is identified, one of the major process improvement methodologies can be applied. Six Sigma is the most predominant and effective method being used around the globe. Its disadvantage is the possibility of optimizing process performance based on an internal view of the organization as opposed to what is important to customers. Another major process improvement methodology is Rummler-Brache. Although easier to use, and a technique that requires customer input and an understanding of customer requirements as its foundation, it lacks solid techniques to measure process performance. Information technology and system solutions should be explored as a way to enhance and strengthen processes but should not dictate or drive the solution of the data needs of the process.

REFERENCES

(1) Malcolm Baldrige National Quality Award, United States Department of Commerce News, February 1999 issue, United States Department of Commerce, Technology Administration, National Institute of Standards and Technology, Baldrige National Quality Award Program, Administration Building, Room A635, 100 Bureau Drive, Stop 1020, Gaithersburg, Maryland 20899-1020, USA. http://www.nist.gov/

(2) Steve Hoisington, "Information and Analysis at IBM's AS/400 Division," published in proceedings from Celebrating Quality, the 10th Annual Minnesota Quality Conference, Saint Paul, Minnesota, USA, October 14, 1998.

(3) "Customer Centered Six Sigma: Linking Customers, Process Improvement, and Financial Results," ASQ Quality Press, Milwaukee, Wisconsin, USA, 2001, by Earl Naumann and Steven H. Hoisington.

(4) Healthcare Financial Management Association, the New Jersey Chapter News Magazine, USA, October 2001, "Six Sigma in Healthcare," by Steve Hoisington.

(5) Steve Hoisington, "Customer Input Guiding Your Six Sigma Initiative," published in proceedings from the ASQ Six Sigma Forum, Chicago, Illinois, USA, 4-5 October 2001.

(6) Ibid.

(7) Geary A, Rummler and Alan P. Brache, Rummler-Brache Group's Process Improvement and Management methodology (now Pritchett), 5800 Granite Parkway, Suite 450, Plano, Texas 75024, USA. 972-731-1500.

REVIEWING PERFORMANCE PROGRESS RELATIVE TO PLANS

Our discussion has focused on a number of proven approaches and initiatives that an organization can use to assess its overall effectiveness and the health of its performance. All of these approaches provide an organization with a list of areas of opportunities, weaknesses, or vulnerabilities in which to improve. It would be criminal to not act upon this data. In fact, failing to act on such data has resulted in several organizations going out of business.

Leadership commitment to improvement, accountability, and alignment is a key ingredient to managing organizational improvement. Leaders should create or foster a culture where improvement is expected and desired behaviors are rewarded. For instance, one of the five core values that have stood the test of time at Johnson Controls, Inc., is "continuous improvement and innovation." A continuous improvement philosophy is so important that it warrants its own value that is documented, communicated, and practiced throughout the organization on an ongoing basis. Leaders also need to hold key members within the organization responsible for achievement of results and continual improvement. Status quo should not be tolerated. Finally, all members in the organization should know how their actions contribute to the overall success or failure of organizational objectives. For example, if an individual struggles with understanding how his or her actions contribute to improving customer satisfaction, the job should be viewed as not adding value.

MONITORING AND MANAGING PROGRESS ON IMPROVEMENT INITIATIVES

There are a number of methods for tracking and monitoring progress relative to plans. A few of the more famous methods are discussed below. However, it is important to remember that the methods used must fit the culture of the organization, be easy to read and understand, and be readily available and accessible. After all, if individuals in the organization do not see progress relative to results, they cannot help address issues. Too many measures, or measures that need explanation, do not help an organization improve. One method that organizations use is to color code results as red, green, or yellow, just like a traffic signal. This technique is sometimes referred to as a Stoplight report or as a Dashboard. The idea is to color code results, both current levels against goals and trends over time, based upon some degree of goodness. Those results that are performing better than expected would be color coded green, like the "go" signal on a traffic light. Little management attention would be warranted for a performance parameter that is functioning as expected. A measurement that is performing a little under what is expected would be color coded yellow, much like a warning signal on a traffic light. This could be for a measurement that is performing close to goal, but the trend is adverse over time. Finally, those measurements that are not performing as expected would be color coded red, like the "stop" signal on a traffic light. Red and yellow coded measurements would warrant further investigation.

Another similar technique is the use of arrows to depict degrees of "goodness." An "up" arrow would indicate a measurement that is performing better than expected. A horizontal arrow, with heads on both ends, would depict a measurement that is performing as expected. And a "down" arrow would depict a measurement that is not performing as expected.

Any of these techniques can be used by an organization to provide a quick snapshot and analysis of organization performance and progress relative to plans. The idea is to keep things simple, provide a methodology that is easy to understand, and allow the organization to prioritize efforts on those areas that warrant attention.

Some of the improvement initiatives discovered by or bestowed on an organization will not be so easy to measure. These might be suggestions for process, policy, and procedure changes. In these cases, the organization should establish some type of format and review mechanism that asks an assigned owner for a status report on a regular basis. An example of such a form is shown in Figure 9.1.

WEEKLY PROBLEM TRACKING REPORT

Problem tracking number:

Owner: Assigned Date:

Problem description:

Root cause analysis:

Proposed solution(s):

Actions to be taken (by whom, when):

Status:

Date resolved:

Verification of effectiveness and sustainability:

Fig. 9.1 Example of Project Status Tracking Form

The idea is that the problem is defined, an owner is assigned, root cause analysis is conducted, and a series of actions are defined to address the issue. Progress toward meeting and implementing these actions should be reviewed along the way at regularly scheduled status meetings.

DEFINING REVIEWS AT DIFFERENT LEVELS OF THE ORGANIZATION

Each part of the organization has a role to play in the overall results of the organization. If the organization fails, all parts of the organization have failed, and vice versa. Therefore, it is necessary for the organization to define a set of performance metrics that predicts its success or failure. These set of measurements should cascade down the organization to each department or organizational structure and individual. Hoshin Planning is one method that aligns individual performance with that of the organization as a whole.

Hoshin Planning

Hoshin Planning is a method of aligning the goals and performance of all employees around an organization's strategic goals. The term "Hoshin" is Japanese for "policy." For those of us outside Japan, the term "goal" is perhaps a better translation. The underlying assumption is that an organization's policy should guide individual performance and that everyone in the organization should be able to clearly see how their work effort and output contributes to achievement of the organization's strategies, goals, and objectives. The application of Hoshin Planning in an organization does not require a one-to-one match for every strategy and goal at all levels. However, all major goals for lower levels should relate to some of the strategic goals. The implication is that each unit or function contributes to some of the strategic goals in a unique way.

Hoshin Planning requires the organization to develop an overall, annual strategic plan. Each business unit and level of the organization derives their Hoshins from the overall strategic plan. Simply stated, each unit within the organization develops goals that support the division's strategy. Each functional area or department develops its goals from the unit's Hoshins. And each employee derives his or her personal performance goals from the functional area or department Hoshins. The performance of every single employee is measured against the Hoshin goals.

By using Hoshin Planning, everyone in the organization knows how their job contributes to the organization. They know how they fit in. Everyone in the organization knows their performance objectives, how they will be evaluated against these, and how their objectives contribute to achievement of overall company strategies, goals, and objectives. Hoshin Planning is a very successful method to institutionalize changes in an organization, align goals and objectives, and institute a culture of responsibility and accountability. Figures 9.2A, 9.2B and 9.2C illustrate a Hoshin Planning approach used by the quality department at Johnson Controls, Inc., Controls Business. The Controls Business Quality Organization's mission, goals, and strategies are aligned with the corporate vision, mission, goals, and strategies.

Organization-Wide Reviews

After performance measurements have been determined for each department and individual in the organization it is important to keep in mind that responsibility and accountability for achievement of the measurements have to be vested with the right people or groups. Oftentimes, an organization assigns measurements to an individual or unit that has no authority or accountability to accomplish the desired results and instead, depends on other parts of the organization to do their job first.

Once a set of performance metrics have been defined for all individuals and parts of the organization, a formal review structure must also be put in place. Typical reviews begin at the top of the organization with all-day meetings to analyze operational performance. These meetings focus on the results achieved in the current period as well as the trend in performance over time. Many organizations refer to these as operations meetings. As a prelude to these meetings, functional heads hold review meetings of their respective departments to assess performance and roll-up results for the operations meeting. These reviews need to be carried out more

Controls Business Quality Organization

VISION/MISSION:

The **Vision** for the Controls Business Quality organization is "Undisputed image of world-class quality leadership of our products and services with our employees, customers, shareholders, and the public as a whole."

This will be accomplished by the following **Mission**: "Ensuring quality and customer satisfaction are key factors influencing tactical business and product/service decisions, and by positively impacting and influencing strategic business and product decisions that affect future quality and customer satisfaction results."

The Controls Business Quality Organization supports SP and SS locations worldwide.

Strategies for accomplishing the Vision/Mission:

1. Ensure key measurements, reports, and reviews are in place, which are customer or business based, that allow Controls Business personnel to predict or react to issues, and that drive quality improvement behavior.

2. Maintain or gain, and efficiently manage certification to any required customer/ industry standard (e.g., agency registration, ISO 9000, UL, CSA in North America), and provide expertise and guidance on worldwide agency certification requirements.

3. Provide or manage audits, assessments, and/or reviews of compliance and readiness initiatives, products/services, processes, or procedures as required or requested.

4. Influence behavior of customers, executives, and employees through communication of Controls Business quality/customer satisfaction posture and improvement activities.

5. Provide expertise and guidance in current and emerging quality practices by sharing knowledge and assisting organizational improvement and learning.

6. *Develop and broadly deploy initiatives and activities that allow Controls Business to achieve Six Sigma commitments to our shareholders and the Corporation.*

7. Influence business process definition and management, procedures and documentation, and measurements that drive commonality, completeness, and integration across Controls Business operations worldwide.

8. *Develop and broadly deploy initiatives and activities that assess our customer satisfaction performance posture, including our position within the industry and against competition, and that lead to improved customer satisfaction, market share, and revenue results.*

9. Manage escalated customer problems and issues to resolution, ensuring all problems are resolved to our customers expectations and that Controls Business executives and employees are aware of current customer issues and our complaint posture.

10. Efficiently and effectively manage all resources, maintaining a highly motivated workforce.

Fig. 9.2A Example of Hoshin Planning Deployment of the Quality Strategy of Controls Business, Johnson Controls, Inc., to the Quality Organization

Controls Business Quality Organization

Mission: Ensuring quality and customer satisfaction are key factors influencing tactical business and product/service decisions, and positively impact and influence strategic business and product decisions that affect future quality and customer satisfaction results.

Goal 6: Develop and broadly deploy initiatives and activities that allow Controls Business to achieve Six Sigma commitments to our shareholders and the Corporation.

Measurements:
- Work with organizational deployment leaders on identifying Six Sigma improvement opportunities that allow Controls Business to meet its corporate commitments
  - Allocate, and gain commitment on waste elimination targets by Controls Business organization by 03/01/XX
  - $XXM in committed identified improvement opportunities, fully achieved by 09/30/XX
- Identify and deploy Six Sigma training needs for all organizations that allow them to achieve commitments
  - XX trained champions by 01/15/XX
  - XX trained black belts by 06/30/XX
  - Employee Six Sigma awareness training developed and deployed to all employees by 03/01/XX
- Establish and deploy measurements of progress and success
  - Publish results to Controls Business executives as part of the Controls Business quality report
- Establish progress reviews with organizational executives (individually) and with Controls Business executives (collectively)

Fig. 9.2B Example of Hoshin Planning Deployment of the Quality Strategy of Controls Business, Johnson Controls, Inc., to the Quality Organization

frequently than the operations meetings. Operations meetings are typically held quarterly, or bi-monthly. Conducting them more frequently serves no purpose as the results of actions taken cannot usually be seen in month-to-month results. For example, an organization may cut expenses associated with headcount. However, such expenses remain in the books for a month or two even after an

Controls Business Quality Organization

Mission: Ensuring quality and customer satisfaction are key factors influencing tactical business and product/service decisions, and positively impact and influence strategic business and product decisions that affect future quality and customer satisfaction results.

Goal 8: Develop and broadly deploy initiatives and activities that assess our customer satisfaction posture, including our position within the industry and against competition, and that lead to improved customer satisfaction, market share, and revenue.

Measurements:
- Develop and conduct customer satisfaction surveys worldwide
    - Create a forum for sharing customer satisfaction results with Controls Business executives and employees on a regular basis
- Quarterly customer satisfaction report
- Quarterly area issues/action reviews
- Be the champion for Control Business customer satisfaction
- Devise, propose, and sell an updated SSNA Scorecard that reflects desired behaviors on customer satisfaction improvement and aligns area customer satisfaction results with area scorecard results by 04/01/XX
- Develop a methodology that allows areas easy access to customer satisfaction data and allows for easy manipulation of data for maximum usage
    - Create and deploy tool by 03/01/XX
    - Success based upon user input on usability
- Advocate changes that will improve customer satisfaction and loyalty worldwide
    - Create methods to "sell" the importance of customer satisfaction to employees and executives
    - Include customer satisfaction targets as part of the overall strategy by 03/01/XX
- Ensure complete communication of customer satisfaction issues, results, and actions
    - Develop a customer satisfaction newsletter by 04/01/XX that sells customer satisfaction improvement and results for SSNA and customers
- Improve customer satisfaction results
    - XX% improvement year-to-year

Fig. 9.2C Example of Hoshin Planning Deployment of the Quality Strategy of Controls Business, Johnson Controls, Inc., to the Quality Organization

individual has left the organization. Severance pay, accrued vacation pay, and other entitlements may remain in the books for several months.

As discussed under Hoshin Planning, an organization can increase the effectiveness of its performance management system by aligning goals throughout the organization. As such, individuals too have goals that support the overall organization's goals and success. Typical employee performance reviews are conducted on an annual basis, hopefully in sync with the organization's business calendar. For instance, if an organization closes its books at the end of a calendar year (December 31), individual performance reviews should be conducted shortly after that date, aligning individual performance with overall organizational results.

Baldrige Reviews

The 2004 version of the Malcolm Baldrige National Quality Award criteria raises several questions regarding organizational-wide reviews.[1] Item 1.1, for instance, questions the way senior leaders in the organization review organizational performance, how they use these reviews to assess organizational success and progress to goals, and how they use these reviews to address changing organizational needs. In addition, the criteria, without being prescriptive, asks for a definition of key performance measures, and how they are deployed throughout the organization, to suppliers and partners, to "ensure organizational alignment." Item 2.2 asks for a description of action plans to address organizational goals and strategies; performance projections for the future; and how performance projections compare against relative comparison points such as industry averages, competition, or other relevant benchmarks. Item 4.1 asks for a description of how review findings are analyzed and communicated to work group and functional-level operations to support decision making. Tying everything together, Category 7 asks for results achieved on the organization's performance management system, all results segmented by all relevant parts of the organization, including work group and functional-level operations and key suppliers and partners.

Chapter 3 discusses the use of the Baldrige criteria to assess organizational performance. In a typical Baldrige assessment, a unit will receive a formal feedback report on its strengths and opportunities for improvement (or weaknesses). Typically, a unit will receive three to five strengths and opportunities per criteria item. Assuming that an organization will focus on improving its weaknesses, and the fact that there are 19 items in the 2004 Baldrige criteria,[2] this means an organization will have to focus on 57 to 95 improvement opportunities.

Several organizations form a team of experts to assemble the (written) application for assessment against the Baldrige criteria. The pamplet "Getting Started with the Baldrige National Quality Program"[3] describes an ideal scenario in which a leader is assigned to each of the seven Baldrige categories to act as an overall coordinator. This single focal point per category allows for consistency in key themes and messages. Assuming this scenario works for assembling a (written) application, the same scenario should work to analyze, dissect, and begin the improvement process. After all, the best person to be assigned ownership for addressing the improvement opportunities is the person most knowledgeable about the content of the written application for that category. This seems a logical way to effectively manage 57 to 95 improvement opportunities.

Another effective way to address improvement opportunities is to combine similar thoughts into one large opportunity statement. In other words, the organization should look for common themes throughout the opportunity statements and develop a newer, and smaller set of improvement opportunities. Oftentimes, a team of examiners that assesses an organization using the Baldrige criteria will do the same thing as part of an exercise to develop themes about an organization. This should yield a more manageable number of opportunities, but they will be larger and more global in nature.

Some examples of key themes might be:

- Lack of continuous improvement efforts across the organization, evident in flat performance trends, absence of systematic reviews, and processes that have remained unchanged for a long period of time.
- Lack of maturity of approaches adopted, demonstrated by a lack of cycles of refinement on processes, initiatives, and strategies.

- No focus on stretch targets or industry leadership as evidenced by a lack of competitive, industry, or comparison data, or other relevant attempts to benchmark operations and process performance.

- Limited deployment of approaches to all parts of the organization, including all employees at all locations.

- Missing integration of key approaches and initiatives as evidenced by a number of strategies and action plans that do not seem to support any common themes or overall strategy.

- Internally focused, optimizing results for the good of the organization as opposed to understanding the impact of operations, processes, and products on customers.

Regardless of the approach taken to address improvement opportunities identified by the Baldrige assessment process, an organization should devote time and attention to making improvements based upon the findings. Sometimes, an organization will spend ergs of energy disputing the findings, stating that the examiners did not understand their business. However, in nearly every case, after some soul searching, organizations discover that the findings were indeed relevant. Over 88 percent of applicants for the Malcolm Baldrige National Quality Award program state that the formal feedback received on their organization was relevant or very relevant, and that it was a very good to excellent investment.[4] An example of a Baldrige feedback report can be found at the Baldrige National Quality Program website (http:www.quality.nist.gov) as part of the annual case study.[5]

TRACKING PROGRESS RELATIVE TO THE BALANCED SCORECARD

Chapter 6 describes how a Balanced Scorecard is developed to help an organization align meaningful and effective organizational measurements with its strategic plan. The philosophy behind a Balanced Scorecard is quite simple. Since mission and vision statements usually have various dimensions and implications across a variety of stakeholders (e.g., employees, shareholders, suppliers, communities, etc.), performance management should also have various dimensions. To assess its performance, an organization should not have to, nor be expected to, review hundreds or thousands of measurements on a regular basis. Likewise, there are not just one or two measurements that can provide this same assessment. However, there are a handful of measurements that are true reflectors of a company's overall performance and are aligned with the company's vision, mission, and strategies.

Summarizing Chapter 6, Robert Kaplan and David P. Norton developed a Balanced Scorecard approach that is described in a number of Harvard Business Review articles.[6] The concept of a Balanced Scorecard suggests that there are four major categories of performance that should be addressed when an organization assesses its overall performance. These are:

1. Financial

2. Customer

3. Internal Business Processes

4. Learning and Growth

Collectively, key measurements in these four areas provide an organization a "balanced" view of performance and not one that is based on financial performance alone.

The **financial** category could include performance metrics such as return on investment, economic value added, revenue growth, profitability, or cash flow. Some organizations may want to include market indicators such as market share as a financial metric, while others may include these under the "customer" category, or even create a separate category for market-oriented dimensions. This "market" category might also include metrics for the rate of new product introduction and innovation. Some organizations may include cost reduction and productivity improvements as financial metrics while other organizations might include such measures as internal, operating indicators, along with cycle time reduction. It is important to remember that classifying performance metrics into one of four major categories may be difficult for an organization. However, the selected performance metrics should be aligned with its vision, mission, and strategies. Linking the Malcolm Baldrige

National Quality Award criteria[7] with the Balanced Scorecard concept, suggestions or hints on meaningful financial-related performance measurements for an organization can be found in the Categories for Strategic Planning (Category 2 in the 2004 criteria); Measurement, Analysis, and Knowledge Management (Category 4 in the 2004 criteria); and in Business Results (Category 7, Item 7.3 in the 2004 criteria).

Customer measures could include customer satisfaction, loyalty or retention rates, customer acquisition, customer profitability, and complaint rates. In practice, the satisfaction level could be derived from an individual customer satisfaction survey question such as overall satisfaction or value for money. It could also be measured by the use of a satisfaction index consisting of three to six questions that are strong predictors of customer satisfaction. Loyalty and retention rates are more difficult to determine for products with long life cycles, but easy to evaluate for ongoing service contracts. Customer acquisition could be indicated by the number of new accounts opened, or the percentage of proposals submitted to prospective customers. Customer metrics could also include measurements such as warranty expenses or warranty claims, since these directly impact the customer's experience with an organization's products. Again, it must be remembered that an organization needs to align its performance measurement system with its vision, mission, and strategies. Most commonly, customer metrics include key measurements such as improvements in customer satisfaction scores, volume or percentage of additional customer business, and reduction in customer complaint rates and warranty expenses. Linking the Malcolm Baldrige National Quality Award criteria[8] with the Balanced Scorecard concept, suggestions or hints on meaningful customer-related performance measurements can be found in the Categories for Customer and Market Focus (Category 3 in the 2004 criteria); Measurement, Analysis, and Knowledge Management (Category 4 in the 2004 criteria); and in Business Results (Category 7, Item 7.1 in the 2004 criteria).

The **internal business process** category could include measures of innovation in products, services, and processes. In practice, however, the two most common metrics for inclusion here are cycle time reduction and productivity improvement. Waste, scrap, defection rates, rework, and quality levels could also be included as internal metrics in this category. In some organizations, supply chain metrics are also viewed as internal operational metrics. The supply issues could include a whole range of material, cycle time, and service issues. Linking the Malcolm Baldrige National Quality Award criteria with the Balanced Scorecard concept, suggestions or hints on meaningful internal business process-related performance measurements for an organization can be found in the categories for Process Management (Category 6 in the 2004 criteria); Measurement, Analysis, and Knowledge Management (Category 4 in the 2004 criteria); and in Business Results (Category 7, Item 7.5 in the 2004 criteria). Dr. James Evans of the Department of Quantitative Analysis and Operations Management, College of Business Administration, University of Cincinnati, wrote a research paper titled Validating Key Results Linkages in the Baldrige Performance Excellence Model.[9] The paper concludes, using a wealth of research and empirical data, that the use of the Baldrige model seeks to validate strong (business) results as an outcome of high performance management practices. The reporting of such results is in a format that emulates the Balanced Scorecard model.

The fourth category in a Balanced Scorecard is **learning and growth of employees**. Performance metrics in this category could include employee satisfaction, average hours of training per employee, overall education expenses, employee suggestion program participation rates, percentage/amount of employee involvement in teams, or percentage/number of employee certifications by professional organizations. Here, the logic is that, in the long term, all organizations compete with each other based on the knowledge level of employees. In essence, all organizations are knowledge organizations. Many organizations expand the use of this category to include a larger array of employee-related metrics such as absenteeism, injury, and retention rates. These are all indirectly related to an organization's acquisition or retention of employee knowledge and skills. Or an organization may choose to add an additional category that covers employee-related issues beyond growth and learning. Again, it is to be remembered that an organization's human performance metrics need to align and support its strategic objectives. Once again, linking the Malcolm Baldrige

National Quality Award criteria[10] with the Balanced Scorecard concept, suggestions or hints on meaningful employee learning and growth-related performance measurements for an organization can be found in the categories for Human Resource Focus (Category 5 in the 2004 criteria); Strategic Planning (Category 2 in the 2004 criteria); Measurement, Analysis, and Knowledge Management (Category 4 in the 2004 criteria); and in Business Results (Category 7, Item 7.4 in the 2004 criteria).

The challenge for an organization is to design a Balanced Scorecard that reinforces its strategic direction and initiatives. To ensure that the scorecard is taken seriously, executive performance evaluation could also be tied to the scorecard, along with incentive compensation. Next, there are three additional issues that must be addressed when determining how a Balanced Scorecard will be used by an organization to assess progress relative to plans. These are identification of the correct metrics, the relative importance weight given to each metric, and the desired performance level.

The correct metrics to use are dependent upon the organization's vision, mission, strategies, and culture. For example, if an organization has a strong focus on expense reduction, then all metrics should show a relationship to improvement in expenses. If growth is the culture, that measurements should show correlation to this culture of growth. Not every executive or everyone in the organization will agree with each component and metric, but they will probably agree with the concept. Everyone in an organization will be satisfied to regularly review a handful of key metrics that represent various areas of the business and that are displayed on one sheet of paper.

If done correctly, the organization's key stakeholders will have some say in the metrics that are included in the Balanced Scorecard. After all, the Balanced Scorecard is meant to reflect an organization's true overall performance, support the interests of all its key stakeholders, and align metrics to support the organization's vision, mission, and strategies. Many organizations validate their set of Balanced Scorecard metrics with their employees and customers, or at least apply a great deal of diligence to ensure the metrics support the "customer's view" as opposed to an internal view of performance.

Once the metrics have been identified and agreed upon, the relative weights, or importance of each on the scorecard, must be determined. The easiest way to weight the scorecard is to make all categories equal. If there are four major categories, as suggested by Kaplan and Norton's Balanced Scorecard model, each would comprise 25 percent of the overall evaluation. If there are five categories, each would represent 20 percent, and so forth. But if a dimension of the strategy, say, cost reductions, was of particular importance, it could be rated relatively higher due to its strategic importance. An organization can adjust these weights to emphasize the importance of a particular strategy or initiative. For example, an organization may want the weight of Balanced Scorecard categories or metrics that have a greater impact on achievement of Six Sigma goals to help kick-start its Six Sigma deployment efforts. The implication is that the weights among the components should reflect importance of each strategic initiative.

An organization could actually determine the importance of each dimension statistically and use these actual weights as part of its Balanced Scorecard. IBM Rochester used multivariate, statistical analysis to determine that there were only five performance metrics that demonstrated strong correlation to each other and also supported overall financial performance.[11] Using 10 years of data, IBM Rochester determined strong statistical correlation among the following factors—employee satisfaction, productivity, cost of quality, customer satisfaction, and market share. The correlation among these factors is shown in Figure 9.3 and Appendix A.

The third issue relating to the Balanced Scorecard is determining and measuring the desired performance level. The performance level of each metric can be set using a number of methods. For example, an organization might have a goal of 15 percent revenue growth per year. Each business unit would then set a goal of 15 percent, or more, revenue growth. Or an organization could have a goal of a 60 percent top box score on overall customer satisfaction. The organization could then compare actual and planned performance levels on the same metric for different divisions within the organization. Benchmarking performance levels against competition, industry leaders, and other world-class organizations is another method that can be used to set specific performance objectives.

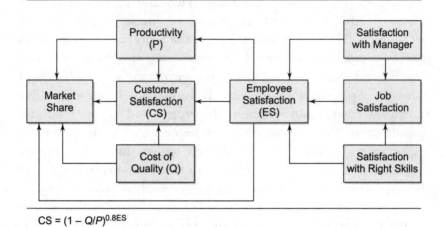

$$CS = (1 - Q/P)^{0.8ES}$$

Fig. 9.3 IBM Rochester Correlation Study on Employee Satisfaction,
Productivity, Cost of Quality, Customer Satisfaction,
and Market Share

Finally, the organization could ask its key stakeholders about their expectations on the Balanced Scorecard performance metrics. This could be done by using a team to develop the appropriate performance metrics.

Once performance levels for the various metrics have been determined, the organization needs to assess performance against these levels. Executive performance evaluations could be based on an integration of all components. In this situation, a single score could be developed from the weights and performance levels for each component. High performance in one area could offset a lower score in another area. Another way to assess overall performance of the complete Balanced Scorecard is to describe some threshold and stretch level of achievement for all the metrics. In other words, an organization may state that for each performance objective, it has established threshold targets that trigger a minimal payout. There could also be stretch goals that trigger a higher level of payout. The exception to this may be financial performance, where the goal is to achieve 100 percent of the target. Another approach is to set threshold and stretch performance levels that **must** be met. This could be applicable to each component. In some organizations, executives need to meet the threshold levels in each area, or else there is no incentive compensation, regardless of performance in other areas. For example, an organization may set a threshold level of 90 percent satisfied (as indicated by top two scores) on the customer satisfaction survey score. If the results are 88 percent satisfied, the executive receives no incentive compensation despite the fact that they may have met the threshold levels on all the other performance metrics. Apart from the threshold performance levels, some organizations set stretch goals and increase the incentive compensation based on the achievement of significantly higher levels of performance above the threshold levels.

From this discussion, it is obvious that a Balanced Scorecard has some very real advantages in reinforcing the desired behavior necessary to achieve a performance level that is in line with strategic objectives and goals. However, it is equally obvious that a Balanced Scorecard must be carefully designed and implemented. Most often, the designing of the scorecard is done by a team of executives who are familiar with the organization's strategy, culture, and overall objectives. Figure 9.4 shows the Balanced Scorecard employed by IBM Rochester.[12] It was developed with the direct assistance of David P. Norton. You will notice that the Balanced Scorecard metrics support key objectives and strategies, as well as the vision and mission statements. Because of the strategic alignment, IBM Rochester developed five categories instead of four. You will also notice that the IBM Rochester Balanced Scorecard metrics support the study described in Appendix A that demonstrates correlation among the factors of employee satisfaction, productivity, cost of quality, customer satisfaction, and market share.

SUMMARY

Organization-wide reviews are necessary to track progress relative to plans. These reviews must begin at the top, with visible senior management support, and permeate down to the lowest level of the organization. Continuous improvement should be the mantra of the organization. For measurement and management systems to be effective, responsibility and accountability for achievement of results must be built into the system.

This book has described a number of methods that can be used to assess the effectiveness and overall health of an organization. The use of the Malcolm Baldrige National Quality Award criteria is one such approach to be used as an overall assessment tool. It is important that an organization effectively uses

IBM ROCHESTER, AS/400 BALANCED SCORECARD

Vision: *TO BRING THE INTEGRATED VALUE OF AS/400 TO e-BUSINESS*

Mission: *Provide high quality systems which enable fast deployment of e-business solutions through superior integration of mainstream technologies and industry leading service and support.*

	Financial/Market Share	Customer/Satisfaction/Loyalty	Product/Channel (Priorities)	Core Processes	People/Skills
GOALS	- Revenue growth that drives improved market share - Industry leading profit margins - Significant growth in new business	- Undisputed leader in customer satisfaction in our industry - Industry leading quality, reliability, and availability - Sustained improvement in customer retention and loyalty - Differentiation through Service and Support	- Rapid deployment of e-business solutions through superior integration of industry leading technologies - Provide product scalability that meets market needs at a competitive price - Improve overall channel productivity and increase number of key Solution Providers and Business Partners - Leadership in Java, collaborative computing, and data warehousing - Competitive e-Commerce, Web serving, and BMS offerings	- Excel as a reliable supplier to our customer, providing products on time and as expected - Improve cost competitiveness and return on investments	- Strengthen our competitive edge in network computing through a high performance culture, characterized by highly skilled, diverse, and motivated people committed to winning in the market place
OBJECTIVES	- Revenue = $X Billion in (year) - Worldwide market share = X% by (year) - Balanced growth of PTI with revenue Greater than 15% revenue from new customers	- Yearly improvement in customer satisfaction gap to competition - Release-to-release product and quality improvement - Continued improvement in key customer satisfaction areas	- Best in industry time-to-deploy e-business - 5000 NC applications by (year) - Price-to-competition gap of 10% by (year) - High-end performance within 10% of competition - Increased channel productivity - Recruit X number of Business Partners by (year) - Competitive Java cost performance and leadership in Java deployment - Cost performance within 20% of Industry leader - Leadership in data warehouse installations	- On-time delivery greater than X% - Responsiveness better than X% - Cost Competitive Index (CCI) better than 0.95 by (year) - Improve inventory turns to X by (year) - Improve hardware warranty expense to revenue (E/R) to X by (year) - Best-in-Industry Time-to-Profit	- Identify and close key skill gaps - Less than 1% attrition in key skills - Improve unit and individual team work scores to X% by (year) - Improve and maintain employee morale by X% - Increase diversity of workforce - % new hires that are women and/or minorities

MEASURES	- Revenue
	- Volumes
	- Market Share by key segments
	- Pre-tax Income
	- Gross Profit
	- Development Expense
	- Brand SG&A
	- New Customer Revenue
		- Worldwide customer Satisfaction score
		- % customer loyalty
		- % customer retention
		- System availability
		- Field hardware quality
		- Software defects
			- Application deployment speed
			- Number of NC and Java applications
			- Price gap to competition
			- High-end performance gap
			- Channel productivity
			- Number of Business Partners recruited
			- Number of data warehouse installs
				- On-time delivery
				- On-time ships
				- Responsiveness
				- Warranty E/R
				- CCI Index
				- Inventory Turns
				- Hardware warranty E/R
				- Time-to-Profit
					- Percent completed skill gaps
					- Percent attrition in key skills
					- Employee survey scores for:
					  — Team work
					  — Morale
					- Percent new hires
					  — Women/Minorities

Fig. 9.4 IBM Rochester's Balanced Scorecard

the results of these assessments for improvement. Often times, organizations spend ergs of energy defending the fact that the assessment results are not relevant. Ignoring warning signs for improvement can cause an organization to fail.

There are a number of approaches that can be employed to present data and status relative to plans. The Dashboard or Stoplight method provides an easy view of measures that warrant further attention. Whatever method is selected, it must be simple, easy to read and understand, and allow the organization to prioritize its improvement efforts. Hoshin Planning can be a useful tool in aligning measures throughout the organization, thus ensuring that every employee knows how his or her job contributes to the overall strategic goals of the organization.

The performance of individuals and business units must be measured against the performance goals. This can be done using a Balanced Scorecard for the senior management. A Balanced Scorecard combines performance measurement in a variety of areas such as financial, customer, processes, and human resources. At the individual level too, performance should be measured against strategic goals.

REFERENCES

(1) 2004 Malcolm Baldrige National Quality Award Criteria for Performance Excellence, Baldrige National Quality Program, National Institute of Standards and Technology, Technology Administration, United States Department of Commerce, Administration Building, Room A600, 100 Bureau Drive, Stop 1020, Gaithersburg, Maryland 20899-1020, USA. http://www.quality.nist.gov.

(2) "Why Apply" brochure, Baldrige National Quality Program, National Institute of Standards and Technology, Technology Administration, United States Department of Commerce, Administration Building, Room A600, 100 Bureau Drive, Stop 1020, Gaithersburg, Maryland 20899-1020, USA.

(3) "Getting Started with the Baldrige National Quality Program" brochure, April 2001, Baldrige National Quality Program, National Institute of Standards and Technology, Technology Administration, United States Department of Commerce, Administration Building, Room A600, 100 Bureau Drive, Stop 1020, Gaithersburg, Maryland 20899-1020, USA.

(4) http://www.quality.nist.gov, Baldrige National Quality Program, National Institute of Standards and Technology, Technology Administration, United States Department of Commerce, Administration Building, Room A600, 100 Bureau Drive, Stop 1020, Gaithersburg, Maryland 20899-1020, USA.

(5) Ibid.

(6) "The Balanced Scorecard—Measures that Drive Performance," the Harvard Business Review, January–February 1992, Number 92015, by Robert S. Kaplan and David P. Norton, Harvard Business School Publishing Corporation, Soldiers Field, Boston, Massachusetts, 02163, USA.

(7) 2004 Malcolm Baldrige National Quality Award Criteria for Performance Excellence, Baldrige National Quality Program, National Institute of Standards and Technology, Technology Administration, United States Department of Commerce, Administration Building, Room A600, 100 Bureau Drive, Stop 1020, Gaithersburg, Maryland 20899-1020, USA. http://www.nist.gov.

(8) Ibid.

(9) Dr. James Evans, "Validating Key Results Linkages in the Baldrige Performance Excellence Model" of the Department of Quantitative Analysis and Operations Management, College of Business Administration, University of Cincinnati, Cincinnati, Ohio, 45221-1030, USA .

(10) 2004 Malcolm Baldrige National Quality Award Criteria for Performance Excellence, Baldrige National Quality Program, National Institute of Standards and Technology, Technology Administration, United States Department of Commerce, Administration Building, Room A600, 100 Bureau Drive, Stop 1020, Gaithersburg, Maryland 20899-1020, USA. http://www.nist.gov.

(11) "Customer Centered Six Sigma: Linking Customers, Process Improvement, and Financial Results," ASQ Quality Press, Milwaukee, Wisconsin, USA, 2001, by Earl Naumann and Steven H. Hoisington.

(12) Ibid.

DELIVERING SHAREHOLDER VALUE AND SUSTAINING PERFORMANCE THROUGH EFFICIENT CORPORATE GOVERNANCE

ORGANIZATIONAL GOVERNANCE USING FINANCIAL AND NON-FINANCIAL MEASURES

Throughout this book, the emphasis has been on assessing organizational health and applying tools to improve performance. This book has reinforced the fact that organizational performance means more than just financial results. Both financial and non-financial measures define the overall health and sustainability of an organization, and help set standards for the definition of performance excellence. This concept was reinforced through the Balanced

Scorecard approach (Chapter 6) that set the stage for an organization to work on both these dimensions that are tied to its strategies.

We now shift focus and discuss how an organization should be measured and held accountable for performance related to both financial and non-financial results. Measuring organizations on non-financial performance results is not a new concept, but a paradigm shift that many organizations, industries, stakeholders, and governance systems have yet to fully embrace. Data from research indicates that as many as 36 percent of the Fortune 500 companies not only use this approach but also use it to decide executive bonuses, which will be discussed in a later section.

But just what is meant by organizational governance? In the Conference Board article titled "*Corporate Governance Best Practices,*" Carolyn Kay Brancato and Christian A. Plath define organizational (corporate) governance as a "system of checks and balances between the board, management, and investors to produce an efficiently functioning organization (corporation), ideally geared to produce long-term value."[1] They further define governance as something that is required by stakeholders to protect value and is typically regulated by laws, rules, and formal regulations.

Strategic Performance Monitoring and Management: Using Non-financial Measures to Improve Organizational Governance

Organizations today confront an ever-growing demand to be more accountable. Financial success, as reflected in dividend payments, is no longer enough, not even for the increasing number of shareholders. They, together with the wider community of stake-holders—employees, customers, and the community—want organizations to be socially and environmentally responsible as well. And this wider community is becoming more assertive about the right to be informed and to influence organizational decisions. The importance and role of non-financial performance measures, in providing the boards of directors and the senior management with the information needed for effective organizational governance, has been the topic of discussion over the last decade. While the current system of financial measures based on accounting remains essential for effective organizational governance, it is clearly inadequate on its own. In a survey of the chief executive officers and directors of companies that use the Canadian performance measurement practice assessed the degree to which performance measurements fit with their organization's stated strategic priorities.[2] The most highly rated strategic priorities were to establish good customer relations, to develop the capacity to innovate, respond and reduce time to markets, and to ensure internal operating efficiencies. The survey revealed that the degree of "fit" between performance measurement and strategic priorities is highest in relation to operating efficiencies, product, and service quality and environment regulations, and somewhat lower with respect to intellectual capital, capacity to innovate, customer relations, investor relations, shareholder relations, and public relations.

Non-financial performance measures that are based on an organization's strategic performance management and monitoring (review) system assist the boards of directors to ensure that:

- Appropriate operational and business processes are in place to enhance learning within the organization.

- All key stakeholder interdependencies and relationships are being effectively managed.

- Appropriate disclosure and assurance systems are in place where it would be useful to communicate non-financial performance measures to external stakeholders. This requirement now is a key component of the Sarbanes–Oxley Law Institution in the United States, which is more fully discussed in the next section.

Organizations around the world struggle with these same issues. For example, company directors in India are awakening to the full import of their fiduciary duties to their shareholders. Indeed, most organizations in India accept the importance of tracking the success and performance of their businesses—and an increasing number of these organizations are now using non-financial or strategic measures alongside traditional performance measures to gauge their health. One of the major software companies in India, Infosys, has worked very successfully with the following approach:

Its key stakeholders are the focal point for all activities, actions, and decisions. As such, the company has created a formal, robust, strategic planning process that considers the inputs and requirements of all its key stakeholders. These inputs and requirements are then translated into performance measurements that the organization monitors through its formal Balanced Scorecard. Measures include financial performance, but more importantly, numerous non-financial measurements as well. In fact, the feeling is that achievement of its key non-financial performance measurements will lead to improved financial results. For instance, if Infosys succeeds in being a good corporate citizen that provides a higher standard of living for employees and citizens of a community and acts in a socially responsible manner in all transactions, including ethical behavior and environmental consciousness, then customers will be more willing to do business with Infosys. Thus, increased revenues and profits will result.

Again, in the Conference Board article titled *Corporate Governance Best Practices,* Carolyn Kay Brancato and Christian A. Plath define the requirement for an organization's governance system to report, monitor, track, and manage financial and non-financial or "strategic" performance measurements to its stakeholders and an independent audit agency.[3] The list of suggested measurements, based on best practices, noted after studying many organizations, is shown in Figure 10.1.

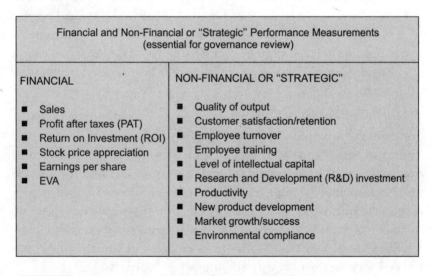

Financial and Non-Financial or "Strategic" Performance Measurements (essential for governance review)	
FINANCIAL	**NON-FINANCIAL OR "STRATEGIC"**
■ Sales	■ Quality of output
■ Profit after taxes (PAT)	■ Customer satisfaction/retention
■ Return on Investment (ROI)	■ Employee turnover
■ Stock price appreciation	■ Employee training
■ Earnings per share	■ Level of intellectual capital
■ EVA	■ Research and Development (R&D) investment
	■ Productivity
	■ New product development
	■ Market growth/success
	■ Environmental compliance

Fig. 10.1 List of Recommended Financial and Non-Financial or "Strategic" Performance Measures to Guide an Organization's Governance System

ORGANIZATIONAL GOVERNANCE GUIDELINES

To help restore investor and public confidence in capital markets, there is an increased emphasis on the accountability of board members and oversight bodies. Many organizations are now working on creating or enhancing a set of formal guidelines to restore and assure confidence of all key stakeholders, including stakeholders, employees, and communities. The Certified Management Accountants of Canada has issued such a guideline that is designed to improve the performance of the boards, CEO's and corporations.[4] It presents a system of measures and processes that, if followed, reduce the potential for or provide early detection of deterioration in an organization's competitive position. The guideline applies the principles of the Balance Scorecard to corporate governance to enable an organization to strengthen its internal and external accountability. As discussed in Chapter 6, the Balanced Scorecard uses both financial and non-financial performance indicators that address an organization's internal business processes, shareholder financial interests, customer value creation, and organizational learning and growth (see Chapter 6). The scorecard approach encourages organizations to focus on setting measurable governance objectives and to report its success in achieving these objectives.

Key features of the Certified Management Accountants of Canada guideline are:

- Processes need to be in place to feed the right type of information to the board that includes strategies and organizational performance.

- Constant efforts to expand the skills and calibre of the board members through appropriate education and training that can be brought to bear during decision making.

- Need for a process to screen and select existing and potential customers to consider broader competencies.

In a Conference Board report published in the May/June 2003 edition of the *Across the Board*, the issue of board incompetence in assessing and assuring the health of an organization is questioned.[5] Other than being of legal age, there are few restrictions on who can serve as a director of a public company. For instance, one does not have to show any minimum competency to read, understand, and comprehend financial statements or an organization's strategies and growth plans. Although many board members are current or former CEO's of major, successful organization, many are simply high-profile individuals who may or may not possess the capacity and experience to provide competent oversight and direction to an organization. For instance, some board members are former politicians, distinguished local citizens, consultants, athletic stars, and school deans or professors. In addition, most current and potential board members are handpicked by the management, the CEO, or the board members, based on personal and professional relationships and friendships established over time. It is extremely rare that a nominated member for the board does not get elected. With this type of arrangement, it is impossible to assure independent and unbiased decisions. Finally, a few board members either personally or indirectly, through their employer, may have vested interests in the financial situation of the organization in which they are board directors. For instance, a board member may own substantial holdings or shares of stock in an organization. Again, with this type of arrangement, independent and unbiased decisions are impossible.

The Conference Board article suggests the following actions to ensure that board directors are competent and that the board operates with independence:

- Preapproval of nominations by the Securities and Exchange Commission (SEC)
- Mandatory, ongoing director education
- Corporate disclosure of the rationale for making a board member nomination
- Pointed corporate disclosure of all board relationships
- Total and post-retirement term limits
- Limitations on concurrent board memberships

The Sarbanes-Oxley Act in the United States has forced many organizations to certify results, both financial and non-financial. This ensures that they develop competent governance systems. Corporate officers and independent auditors, and in some cases board members, must sign a statement that guarantees the accuracy of reported results. Automatically, this assigns accountability for results of the organization and extends this responsibility beyond just financial reporting. The Sarbanes-Oxley Act takes the responsibility for accurate reporting of results one major step further, and requires certification of the processes that yield the results. Therefore, there is no questioning how the results were achieved or derived.

H. Mathiesen has described a typical system of management and oversight (governance) that depicts, in Figure 10.2, the flow of information, associated issues, and breakdown in accountability.[6] Figure 10.2 shows how an organization and its management, principals, and agents are impacted by the effects of both financial and non-financial performance. The boxes at the bottom of Figure 10.2 identify examples of conditions, mechanisms, and costs associated with such a structure. It is interesting to note that many of the issues are caused by a lack of understanding of the organization's strategies, as well as disagreement on associated strategic objectives— the very problem the Balanced Scorecard attempts to address. This further reinforces the importance of aligning the organization's management and its governance structure with the organization's strategy and objectives. If there is disagreement, lack of understanding, or lack of competence in understanding the organization's existence, then conflict will result that will hamper the organization.

EXECUTIVE COMPENSATION

Executive compensation has been under constant scrutiny as major stakeholders have more information on which to base their assessment and opinions. Major stakeholders include shareholders who expect dividends and stock value to be commensurate with executive compensation, and employees who measure their pay increases against those given to the organization's executives. If sales are off, and stock prices stall or fall, and dividends remain flat or decline, shareholders do not expect executives to receive bonuses. Likewise, if employees receive a four percent annual pay increase, they expect their senior executives to receive a similar percentage increase, not increases that are two to 100 times higher than the rest

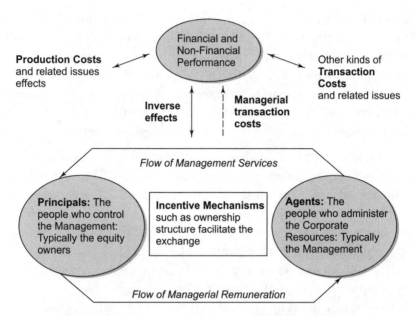

Examples of conditions, mechanisms and managerial transaction costs

TRANSACTION CONDITIONS	INCENTIVE MECHANISMS	MANAGERIAL TRANSACTION COSTS
Environment conditions • Asymmetric information • Complexity/uncertainty • Difficulty in measuring • Asset specificity • Duration/frequency • Behavioral conditions • Opportunism • Bounded rationality • Risk aversion	• Decision systems • Performance monitoring systems • Remuneration systems • Bankruptcy systems • Ownership structures • Creditor structures • Capital structures • Market for corporate control • Market for management services • Product market competition	• Monitoring costs • Perquisite consumption • Pet projects • Free cash flow dispersion • Hampered capital access • Replacement resistance • Resistance to profitable liquidation or merger • Power struggles • Excessive risk taking • Self-dealing transfer pricing • Excessive diversification • Excessive growth

Fig. 10.2 The Managerial Agency Problem

of the employees. Executive compensation is touted by most organizations to be tied to financial performance of the organization, yet there is little correlation. For instance, while the overall Gross National Product in the United States dropped 12 percent in 2002 and stock prices decline more than 27 percent, executive compensation rose 10.3 percent.[7]

As discussed throughout this book, there is a movement underway to assess overall performance of an organization based on non-financial performance as well as financial performance. More and more stakeholders are demanding that non-traditional and non-financial measurements be used to assess executive compensation. There is little need to overemphasize the fact that for the success of any program or major initiative such as deployment of Six Sigma, high scoring Baldrige application, achievement of ISO 9000 registration, or achievement of a certain SEI/CMM level, connecting executive bonuses to the results has a better chance of success relative to deployment and adding value to the organization. In a 1995 study from Wharton Business School in Pennsylvania, 36 percent of the organizations surveyed used non-financial measures to determine executive rewards.[8] More enlightening from the study was the revelation that organizations that pursued strategies founded on innovation and new product development—strategies that are fundamentally long-term in scope—tended to favor non-financial measures, and organizations whose shares were owned by external board members were the ones to favor non-financial measures.

As discussed earlier, tools such as the Balanced Scorecard provide a means for the organization to look at high impact, non-financial measures to assess the overall health and sustainability of an organization. And executive compensation should also be tied to achievement of overall results. In the Controls business of Johnson Controls, Inc., executive compensation is based on the achievement of a combination of financial and non-financial measures.[9] These include revenue growth (percent), profits before taxes (actual percent and total amount), customer satisfaction results, Six Sigma results, safety (incident rate), and employee morale. Each factor is assigned a target goal and weight. For example, revenue growth represents 20 percent of the total bonus percent, profits represent 30 percent, customer satisfaction represents 20 percent, Six Sigma results represents 10 percent, safety results represent 10 percent, and employee morale represents 10 percent. IBM Rochester based executive compensation on a similar approach, but also added incentives for achievement of specific initiatives.[10] For instance, achievement of ISO 9000 and 14000 registrations were built into the executive compensation programs in the years in which these initiatives were expected to be achieved. Achievement of the special initiatives carried a weight of 10 percent of the total bonus percent. This is a "go, no-go" type of attainment. If ISO 9000 or 14000 was achieved in the month planned, then the variable portion of executive compensation would be increased by 10 percent. If not achieved in the month planned, then no additional increase would be added. The caveat in paying for achievement of non-financial results is that the financial results have to be achieved first, before the bonus structure for the non-financial results takes affect.

Appendix A demonstrates the actual correlation between employee satisfaction, productivity, cost of quality, and customer satisfaction at IBM Rochester. Revenue and profitability are built into several of the factors already (e.g., productivity is measured as revenue per employee). More and more stakeholders are understanding the correlation between non-financial performance and overall long-term financial performance and sustainability of an organization. Earl Naumann and Steven H. Hoisington dedicate an entire chapter (Chapter 2) in the book titled *Customer Centered Six Sigma: Linking Customers, Process Improvement, and Financial Results* to a discussion of the correlation between non-financial measurements and financial results.[11] Many of the non-financial measurements are leading indicators of future financial performance of the organization.

CORPORATE GOVERNANCE AND BALDRIGE

The Malcolm Baldrige National Quality Award criteria added a focus on organizational governance in 2003, after several abuses by large corporations in 2002 and 2003 because of little or no oversight.[12] As part of the assessment of the Organizational Leadership (system) in Category 1 of the Baldrige criteria, organizational governance requirements were added to address the need for a responsible, informed, independent, and accountable governance body that is capable of addressing the interests of the key stakeholders of the organization. Specifically, the criteria ask the organization in Item 1.1 how its governance system addresses:

- management accountability for the organization's actions
- fiscal accountability
- independence of internal and external audits, and
- protection of stockholder and stakeholder interests

Item 1.2 questions the organization's key processes and measures or indicators for monitoring ethical behavior throughout the organization. There are no canned answers and the beauty of the Baldrige criteria is that it gets an organization to ponder over the optimal approach if its current approach seems inadequate.

Category 1 of the Baldrige criteria also asks how the organization reviews performance and capabilities, and how these reviews are used to assess organizational success. In other words, the criteria asks how the organization looks at financial and non-financial aspects of its operations to determine how well it is performing. The criteria goes on to question which key performance measures are reviewed on a regular basis and how the organization evaluates the performance of senior leaders and members of its board of directors (as appropriate) on results achieved by the organization on key performance measurements. In essence, the criteria imply the accountability for achievement of results lies with senior leaders and board members. In addition, the criteria imply that the results reported need to be honest and accurate.

As referenced in Chapter 9, Dr. James Evans of the Department of Quantitative Analysis and Operations Management, College of Business Administration, University of Cincinnati, wrote a research paper titled *Validating Key Results Linkages in the Baldrige Performance Excellence Model*.[13] The paper concludes, using a wealth of research and empirical data, that use of the Baldrige model seeks to validate strong (business) results as an outcome of high performance management practices, and the reporting of such results is in a format that emulates the Balanced Scorecard model. Dr. Evans suggests that the Baldrige approach be used as a model to assess overall organizational health and should be a practice that is highly encouraged or required as part of the organization's independent governance system.

OVERALL ASSESSMENT OF ORGANIZATIONAL GOVERNANCE EFFECTIVENESS

In a recent Conference Board paper titled *Executive action—does your Board have an effective management system of its own?*, the authors advocate a three-step assessment process[14]:

1. Short-term compliance review

Does the board follow prudent and best practices in the area of auditing, disclosure of related party transactions, and reporting of special transactions?

2. Overall board assessment

Does the organization have a board which will take it where it wants (and needs) to go? Does the organization have a process for measuring the Board's performance? This step is centered around understanding and assessing the adequacy of a long-term strategy which is consistent with the proposal to develop and deploy a set of measures linked to the strategy of the organization.

3. Individual member assessment

Does the organization have the right mix of skills on the board? Is the organization satisfied with individual member contributions?

In a Harvard Business Review article titled *Assessing Board Room Performance,* the authors cite an example of Motorola using multiple choice questions in an internal survey to evaluate the board's effectiveness.[15] A sample is shown in Figure 10.3.

There are a number of measurements that organizations are contemplating on using to assess the effectiveness of governance. The perfect measurement, or set of measurements, has not yet been developed or proposed. However, effectiveness of governance on an organization will be as individualized as the organization itself. What organizations and its stakeholders are discovering, however, is that looking only at financial performance is not enough. Some examples of measurements or assessments that organizations and its stakeholders can use to assess the effectiveness of organizational governance include:

The Board of Directors	Strongly Agree	Agree	Neither Agree nor Disagree	Disagree	Strongly Disagree
Board member nominations have pre-approvals from SEC					
CEO evaluations are data driven					
Have sufficient understanding of the organizational processes					
Board members have individual accountabilities and have measures of performance consistent with the scorecard of the organization					
Board members are appointed for their caliber and excellence that add value to the organization					
Changes to organizational structures are backed by data analysis					
Enough time is spent on Board meetings discussing the long-range strategy of the organization					
Members participate actively on judging organization performance on both the financial and non-financial dimensions					

Fig. 10.3 Motorola Internal Survey Example to Evaluate the Board's Effectiveness

- Results from all internal and external audits, including ISO 9000 internal and external audits and SEI/CMM assessments (Chapter 4)
- Financial audit results by independent agencies such as PricewaterhouseCoopers used for Securities and Exchange Commission (SEC) compliance
- Internal financial audit results from independent auditors

- Overall success at achieving Balanced Scorecard measurements

- Customer satisfaction results against targets, competitors, and benchmarks

- Baldrige assessment scores, including success at closing opportunities year-to-year (Chapter 3)

- Governance ratings from independent agencies such as Industry Week, the Securities and Exchange Commission (SEC), or the Institutional Shareholder Services (ISS) organization

SUMMARY

The organizational governance structure is the final arbiter as to whether an organization is meeting its obligations to its stakeholders. The approach to look at more than just financial performance to assess an organization's health and predictability for future success and sustainability has moved into the realm of the organizational governance structure. Studies reveal that 36 percent of the Fortune 500 companies are already focused on a balance of financial and non-financial measures. Several examples of international organizations applying this approach are cited throughout the chapter.

Several guidelines have been developed to help organizations and its stakeholders assess the effectiveness of organizational governance. Some have been developed by industry associations, but at least one has been edicted by law—the Sarbanes-Oxley Act—that requires executives of organizations to certify organizational performance and the processes used to achieve this performance.

Equally important is the requirement that the organization's governance structure must be unbiased and capable of performing an independent assessment of the organization. Board members are not necessarily selected based upon competence, and in many cases, the professional and personal relationships among board members as well as the organization's management make it difficult to maintain a system of independence.

Finally, tools such as the Baldrige assessment, internal and external audits, and results of organizational performance reviews including Balanced Scorecard results should be considered and used by organizations and their governance structure to assess overall performance relative to stakeholder requirements and expectations.

REFERENCES

(1) Kay Brancato and Christian A. Plath, "Corporate Governance Best Practices," the Conference Board, 845 Third Avenue, New York, New York, 10022-6679, USA, Special Report, 2003.

(2) "Strategic Performance Monitoring and Management: Using Non-financial Measures to Improve Corporate Governance," John Waterhouse, Ph.D, Simon Fraser University, and Ann Svendsen, Core Relation Consulting, CA Magazine, USA, March 1999.

(3) Kay Brancato and Christian A. Plath, "Corporate Governance Best Practices," the Conference Board, 845 Third Avenue, New York, New York, 10022-6679, USA, Special Report, 2003.

(4) "Certified Management Accountants of Canada Board Governance Guidelines," Marc Epstein, Distinguished Research Professor of Management at Jones Graduate School of Management at Rice University in Houston, Texas, USA; Toronto, Ontario, Canada, September 2002.

(5) Gary Moreau, "Fixing Corporate Boards", Across the Board magazine, the Conference Board, 845 Third Avenue, New York, New York, 10022-6679, USA, May/June 2003 edition.

(6) H. Mathiesen, "The Managerial Agency Problem," Acad Publishing, Version 2.6, Dvevej 4, DK-2970, Hoersholm, Copenhagen, Denmark, 45-2620-7075, 1997–2003.

(7) Charles Peck, Henry M. Silvert, and Gina McCormick, "Top Executive Compensation in 2002," The Conference Board, 845 Third Avenue, New York, New York, USA 10022-6679, 2003.

(8) Christopher D. Ittner, David F. Larcker, and Madhav Rajan, "The Choice of Performance Measures in Annual Bonus Contracts," Harvard Business Review, USA, Jan/Feb 1996.

(9) Earl Naumann and Steven H. Hoisington, "Customer Centered Six Sigma: Linking Customers, Process Improvement, and Financial Results," published by ASQ Quality Press, Milwaukee, Wisconsin, USA, 2001.

(10) Published in the proceedings from Celebrating Quality, the 10th Annual Minnesota Quality Conference, Saint Paul River Center, Saint

Paul, Minnesota, USA, October 14, 1998, "Information and Analysis at IBM's AS/400 Divison" session by Steve Hoisington.

(11) Earl Naumann and Steven H. Hoisington, "Customer Centered Six Sigma: Linking Customers, Process Improvement, and Financial Results," published by ASQ Quality Press, Milwaukee, Wisconsin, USA, 2001.

(12) Malcolm Baldrige National Quality Award, United States Department of Commerce, United States Department of Commerce, Technology Administration, National Institute of Standards and Technology, Baldrige National Quality Award Program, Administration Building, Room A635, 100 Bureau Drive, Stop 1020, Gaithersburg, Maryland, 20899-1020, USA. http://www.nist.gov.

(13) Dr. James Evans, "Validating Key Results Linkages in the Baldrige Performance Excellence Model" of the Department of Quantitative Analysis and Operations Management, College of Business Administration, University of Cincinnati, Cincinnati, Ohio 45221-1030, USA.

(14) Carolyn Brancato, "In the wake of Enron, does your Board have an effective management system of its own", Executive Action, The Conference Board, 845 Third Avenue, New York, New York, 10022-6679, USA, 2003, Edition Number 14, Februray 2002.

(15) Jay A. Conger, David Finegold, and Edward E. Lawler III, "Appraising Board Performance," Harvard Business Review, Harvard Business School Publication Corporation Boston, Massachusetts, USA, Volume 76, Issue 1, January/February 1998 edition.

CHAPTER ELEVEN

SUMMARY

Organizations exist to serve customers. This point has been stressed numerous times throughout the book. Organizations serve many stakeholders, including shareholders, employees, the community, and, of course, customers. All stakeholder requirements need to be considered if the organization expects to sustain its performance over the long term. Organizations need to learn how to determine, measure, and then deliver consistent stakeholder value.

Business transformation is a requirement for any organization in today's fast-paced environment, and a number of models and methods exist to facilitate organizational change. Organizations need to carefully consider the plethora of tools and techniques that exist to help with change management and be cognizant of the fact that there is no one right tool for every situation. The organization should never lose sight of is values and beliefs, that customers must always come and remain first, and that change is inevitable. This book has presented an integrated approach that explains how to make the best use of the most vogue, available approaches such as the Economic Value Added (EVA), Baldrige-based assessments, Balanced Score Card, Six Sigma, and others. When integrated into a composite transformation program, these approaches deliver value as opposed to their use in a stand-alone mode—a practice deployed by most organizations.

This book has discussed major topics impacting organizations that are grappling with the concept of change management and the need to significantly improve performance. Many organizations, in the context of rapidly changing market dynamics and fierce competition, need to not only be responsive to these changes, they also need to continue to re-strategize on an ongoing basis to maintain their leading edge.

The steps proposed in this book are as follows:

1. Organizations need to create and enhance customer and stakeholder value. Thus, any organizational transformation initiative should focus on identifying areas for improvement and implementing solutions to maximize value. It is important to understand and create a customer-centric environment, which is discussed in Chapter 1.

2. Organizations need to create a strategy that considers the inputs and requirements of all stakeholders, is focused on both the short term and longer term, and aligns objectives and action plans throughout the organization. The true test of an effective strategy is how well it does in generating stakeholder value. Economic Value-Added or EVA is a concept introduced in Chapter 2, which measures the wealth of the organization and, hence, is a direct indicator of stakeholder value.

3. Once an organization has defined its strategy and action plans, it is important to assess how well it is doing on meeting its goals and objectives, as well as delivering stakeholder value. Organizational assessment tools such as the Baldrige or EFQM models, as well as other models discussed in Chapter 3 and Chapter 4, provide insights on the health of the organization as well as areas that are not performing as expected. These models assess the holistic health of the organization and identify strategic gaps and assess the strength of an organization's customer focus and the breadth and alignment of its process management system.

4. Now that opportunities have been identified through the use of an assessment model, it is necessary to prepare the organization for change, and then implement the changes. Environments in which organizations operate are dynamic and constantly changing. And to transform the organization's culture to one that is more customer focused, a formal change management system will be required. Chapter 5 discussed the basic elements required for change within the organization, the dynamics associated with change, and how to prepare for and reinforce change throughout the organization.

5. Organizations need to determine the right combination of financial and non-financial measures to help them monitor performance and assess how well they are doing at delivering stakeholder value as well as closing strategic gaps. Focusing only on financial performance is a short-term approach and will prevent the organization from creating strategies and actions that support the needs of all stakeholders. The Balanced Scorecard (BSC) introduced in Chapter 6 is one tool that enables organizations to arrive at the right combination of measures that are in turn tied to the strategies of the organization. The BSC is one implementation tool that an organization can use to address strategic gaps identified through the assessment process and to align and integrate its improvement efforts throughout the organization. The Balanced Scorecard creates a strategy management framework, which is important for managing key improvement initiatives.

6. The previous steps can now be combined to determine a set of initiatives the organization needs to focus on in order to improve. The organization needs to identify features and processes that support strategies as well as close strategic gaps. This is the internal infrastructure and processes that are aligned with customer (stakeholder) needs. Some of these techniques, described in Chapter 7, include a "Customer Expectations—Process Matrix" and "Quality Function Deployment" (QFD) or "House of Quality" model. These too are implementation tools that the organization can use to address strategic gaps identified through the assessment

process and to align and integrate its improvement efforts. Initiatives need to be launched in the organization to meet the goals and targets for each of the strategic measures quarter over quarter and year over year.

7. Obviously, the next logical step is to prioritize initiatives. Problem-solving tools such as Six Sigma and Rummler-Brache can be used to bring about process improvements based on priorities. All organizations run on processes—some more formal than others. Prioritization, process performance, and problem-solving techniques have been discussed in Chapter 8.

8. With an assessment completed, an organization ready for change, a Balanced Scorecard in place, and improvement tools in hand, the organization then needs to review, track, and manage performance improvement. Chapter 9 provides a number of mechanisms and approaches an organization can use to review progress against plans. Some of these include Dashboard, Stoplight, and Hoshin Planning.

9. The result of all the previous steps would be to see how well the organization has delivered value to its key stakeholders. We have also briefly discussed the importance of organiza-tional governance and how individual board members could be made accountable for guiding the destiny of the organization and maintaining and sustaining shareholder value. Even more important is the understanding that the organization's governance system requires a paradigm shift to judge its performance on both financial and non-financial dimensions. This concept has been discussed in Chapter 10.

In conclusion, global changes, and their dynamics, are asserting themselves in a manner that organizations need to recognize and respond to the changes effectively to stay ahead of the curve. From the industrial age to the information age to increased connectivity facilitated by the Internet, changes are occurring everyday. Change is inevitable. The linkages and the interactions between the chapters are depicted in Figure 7.1. These linkages and interactions form the basis for an overall model to implement strategic change.

CUSTOMER SATISFACTION AND MARKET SHARE—AN EMPIRICAL CASE STUDY OF IBM'S AS/400 DIVISION

THEORY VERSUS FACT

As a society, we are constantly bombarded by theories that we would like to believe are true. We are evolving into a society where managing, based on facts rather than gut feelings, is becoming commonplace. The distinction between theory and fact is quite vast. Take for instance the notion that happy employees produce fewer defects. Or, would one be comfortable allowing disgruntled employees to handle customer service calls? We know in our hearts what is right, but how can we prove this?

A Harvard Business Review article outlines a profit chain theory suggesting a direct relationship between quality, employee satisfaction, employee productivity, customer satisfaction, and revenue growth.[1] Intuitively, the theory makes sense, but can it be proved? Possibly in contemplation of this, David L. Rivera, editor of Continuity, a publication by the Electronics Division Association of the American Society for Quality Control (ASQC), wrote in the Winter 1994 edition that "...if a story demonstrated a strong correlation between employee satisfaction and customer satisfaction, then that would be news."[2]

Business Quality, and People-Related Measurements

IBM's AS/400 Division in Rochester, Minnesota, winner of the 1990 Malcolm Baldrige National Quality Award, struggled with this same dilemma. Management is constantly bombarded with a wealth of information and a plethora of measurements. But which measurements have the greatest impact on overall business performance?

Armed with a fistful of theories and 10 years of data, we set about trying to determine if there are any relationships among the numerous measurements that the organization focuses on. The study included interviewing AS/400 Division managers from various functional organizations. They were asked to identify those measurements they felt were most important. A list of over 50 key measurements were considered. This list included traditional measurements such as market share, overall customer satisfaction, employee morale, job satisfaction, warranty costs, inventory costs, product scrap, and productivity. The list of key measurements can be defined in three general areas: business-related such as revenue and productivity; quality-related such as customer satisfaction and warranty cost; and people-related such as employee satisfaction and morale.

Measurement Correlation Proven

Strong correlation has been demonstrated between the following measurements: market share, customer satisfaction, productivity, warranty cost, and employee satisfaction. Figure A1 illustrates those measurements that have a strong relationship between them as defined by a correlation factor equal or greater than 0.7.

IBM AS/400 Division Data 1984–1994

	Market Share	Customer Satisfaction	Productivity	Cost of Quality	Employee Satisfaction	Job Satisfaction	Satisfaction W/O manager	Right Skills
Marketshare	1.00	0.71	0.97	–0.86	0.84	0.84	- -	0.97
Customer Satisfaction	0.71	1.00	- -	–0.79	0.70	- -	- -	0.72
Productivity	0.97	- -	1.00	- -	0.93	0.92	0.86	0.98
Cost of Quality	–0.86	–0.79	- -	1.00	- -	- -	- -	- -
Employee Satisfaction	0.84	0.70	0.93	- -	1.00	0.92	0.92	0.86
Job Satisfaction	0.84	- -	0.92	- -	0.92	1.00	0.70	0.84
Satisfaction with Manager	- -	- -	0.86	- -	0.92	0.70	1.00	0.92
Right Skills	0.97	0.72	0.98	- -	0.86	0.84	0.92	1.00

Productivity (P) = Revenue per Employee
Cost of Quality (Q) = Hardware Warranty Cost
Employee Satisfaction (ES) = Index of Job Satisfaction, Satisfaction with Manager, and Satisfaction with Right Skills

- To improve **Employee Satisfaction**, then focus on improving **Job Satisfaction, Satisfaction with Manager,** and **Satisfaction with Having the Right Skills for the Job.**
- To improve **Job Satisfaction**, then focus on improving **Satisfaction with Manager** and **Satisfaction with Having the Right Skills for the Job.**
- Improving **Satisfaction with Having the Right Skills for the Job** will improve **Employee Satisfaction, Job Satisfaction,** and will directly impact **Productivity, Marketshare,** and **Customer Satisfaction.**
- Improving **Employee Satisfaction** will directly impact **Productivity** and **Marketshare.**
- To improve **Customer Satisfaction**, then focus on improving **Productivity, Employee Satisfaction,** and decrease the **Cost of Quality.**
- Decreasing the **Cost of Quality** will directly impact **Customer Satisfaction** and **Marketshare.**
- Improving **Customer Satisfaction** will directly impact **Marketshare.**

Fig. A1 Measurement Correlation

Figure A1 illustrates those measurements that have strong relationship between them, as defined by a correlation factor equal to or greater than 0.7.

The following descriptions explain the sources for the measurements found to be strongly correlated:

- Customer Satisfaction (Cs) data is derived from customer satisfaction surveys of AS/400® customers. Cs represents the decimal fraction of the percentage of customers responding "satisfied" or "very satisfied" on the five-point scale surveys.

- Employee Satisfaction (Es) data is derived from an annual survey of AS/400 Division employees. The indicator used is an unweighted index representing the decimal fraction of the percentage of employees responding favorably to a set of survey questions. These survey questions, among other things, address employee satisfaction with their job, their immediate manager, and their level of skills.

- Productivity (P) is computed as the measurement of revenue produced per number of employees, calculated on an annual basis.

- Quality (Q) represents a measurement of the cost of quality. Although numerous measurements of the cost of quality exist, such as scrap and rework expenses, warranty costs (expenses) had the highest correlation to the other measurements used in this study. Warranty costs include labor, parts and service expended during the warranty period of an AS/400. An aggregate of both hardware and software maintenance and service is used in this calculation. This represents the total required costs associated with servicing an AS/400 at a customer's location, including replacement costs. Warranty cost per employee is calculated on an annual basis.

Theories Proven

Figure A2 illustrates the relationship among the factors. Only those measurements with a correlation factor equal or greater than 0.7 are shown. This study can be used to factually prove earlier theories. To improve employee satisfaction, focus on improving job satisfaction,

satisfaction with management, and satisfaction with having the rights skills for the job. To improve job satisfaction, focus on improving satisfaction with management and satisfaction with having the right skills for the job. Improving satisfaction with having the right skills for the job will improve employee satisfaction, job satisfaction, and will positively impact productivity, marketshare, and customer satisfaction. Improving employee satisfaction will directly impact productivity and customer satisfaction and will decrease warranty costs. Decreasing warranty costs will directly impact customer satisfaction and market share. Improving customer satisfaction will directly impact market share.

In theory, these relationships make sense. Satisfied employees should have higher productivity and provide good service to customers. If warranty costs decrease, fewer defects are being passed on to customers, resulting in higher customer satisfaction. Employees who are satisfied that they have the right skills for the job, and with their relationship with the management, should be more satisfied overall.

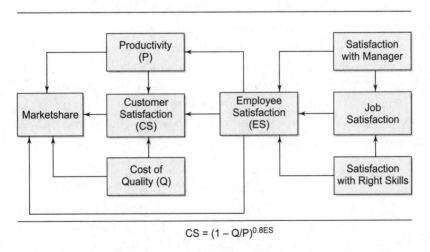

$$CS = (1 - Q/P)^{0.8ES}$$

Fig. A2 Relationship among Factors

Figure A2 illustrates the relationship between Marketshare, Customer Satisfaction, Productivity, Cost of Quality, and Employee Satisfaction.

An Aggregated Approach to Using Measurements

This study was not meant to explore every possible impact or relationship between operational measurements. However, a favorable outcome of this study suggests the need to take an enterprise view of measurements and understand the impact of one measurement on another. Most organizations are hierarchical and functionally oriented. Typically, customer satisfaction, employee satisfaction, quality and productivity are managed by a different group. Therefore, analyses and decisions are generally performed by each separate group, without consideration for overall integration among these measurements. Additionally, reviews of these measurements are typically done through separate meetings or reports. A company needs to understand these relationships and review these measurements in aggregation. Otherwise, actions may be taken that have the opposite effect on upstream results. For instance, if an action impacts employee satisfaction, such as a layoff, the company must consider counteractions to prevent a decline in productivity, customer satisfaction, and marketshare.

Although the results of this study have proved useful for IBM's AS/400 Division, others should be wary of applying the absolute results to their business. The relationships between measurements will vary by industry. Different cost of quality measurements need to be tested. What is important, however, is for an organization to use a systematic approach to understanding the relationship of key operational measurements and review these in aggregate as opposed to entities in themselves.

REFERENCES

(1) "Putting the Service-Profit Chain to Work," Harvard Business Review, March–April 1994, James L. Heskett, Thomas O. Jones, Gary W. Loveman, W. Earl Sasser, Jr., and Leonard A. Schlesinger.

(2) "Customer Satisfaction," Continuity, ASQC-Electronics Division, Issue 97, Winter 1994, David L. Rivera.

® AS/400 is a registered trademark of IBM. Application System/400 and Advanced Series/400 are commercial computers developed and manufactured by IBM's AS/400 Division in Rochester, Minnesota.

Authors:

Steven H. Hoisington
Director, Market-Driven Quality

IBM
3605-Highway 52 North
Rochester, MN 55901

Tze-Hsi (Sam) Huang
Statistician, Customer
Satisfaction Management

IBM
3605-Highway 52 North
Rochester, MN 55901

COMPARISON OF OTHER INTERNATIONAL MODELS SUCH AS ISO 9000 AND TL 9000, QS 9000 TO THE BALDRIGE MODEL

ISO 9000

The ISO 9000 Quality Management System Standards was first released by the International Organization for Standardization in Geneva in 1987. Subsequently, it underwent two revisions—in 1994 and in 2000. When first introduced as a standard, it helped both organizations and customers. When customers bought a product or service from a supplier who was certified to the ISO standard, they were assured of quality. Prior to ISO 9000, several companies came up with a checklist, referred to by many as a Vendor Evaluation Checklist, that consisted of questions trying to understand the quality processes deployed by suppliers. The ISO standard has gained acceptability all over the world, so much so that many organizations now require compliance to the standard as a condition for doing business.

In the 1987 and 1994 versions of the standard, we had three separate standards. ISO 9001 was meant for organizations dealing with design, development, manufacturing, and installation; ISO 9002 was for organizations involved in manufacturing and ISO 9003 was for inspection activities. The latest revision, the ISO 9000: 2000, has only one standard, eliminating the three different standards with a provision in Clause 7 of the new standard, to identify the applicable areas depending on what the organization does as its main operation.

The other major advantage of compliance to the standard is that the quality management system lends itself to scrutiny by an independent party. There are a number of agencies such as DNV, BSI, UL, and others who have the authority to audit and certify an organization to the standard. This unbiased audit has provided lot of credence to the overall ISO process, as exemplified by numerous registrations all over the world.

TL 9000

TL 9000 is specific to the telecommunication industry and is based on the ISO framework. Put together by a joint group of telecom suppliers and service providers called the Quest Forum (Quality Excellence for Suppliers of Telecommunications), the standard was first released in 1998, in line with ISO 1994, and was referred to as version 2.5. Now, the standard is aligned with ISO: 2000 and the version is 3.0.

The difference between ISO and TL is that TL 9000 operates in two parts—requirements and measurements. In fact, there are two separate books for each. In the case of requirements, there are "adders"—as many as 81 of them—imposed on the basic ISO framework. These are specific to the Telecom industry.

In the case of measurements, separate metrics have been identified for hardware, software, and services. The measurement category includes customer satisfaction and problems, fix response time, on time delivery, system outages, software aborts, and hardware returns.

Suppliers can use these measures to improve their business and customer relations. They will report comparable measurements into a secure industry database maintained at the University of Texas-Dallas (UTD) for benchmarking purposes. By establishing a consistent set of comparable measurements, the Quest Forum has scored an industry first, with the goal of improving the Telecom industry.

While ISO focuses on certifying the quality system of any organization, TL 9000 certifies products. The Book on Measurements has provided a figure where it has all the product categories listed (Appendix A1—Figure 1) and Figure A2 has the corresponding metrics identified for each of those product categories.[1] So the first thing to be done by an organization, if it wants to register its company to TL 9000, is to identify what products are being certified, map those products to the product categories in Figure A1 of the handbook, and determine from Figure A2 of the handbook the applicable metrics. Prior to a certification audit, three months of data are required for all those applicable metrics and the auditors generally look for DCRs (Data Confirmation Reports) that the MRS (Metrics Repository System) in UTD will send back to the company seeking registration as confirmation of the fact that the metrics are in order. Following the certification audit, the organization certified has to continue submitting metrics so as to reach UTD no later than the seventh week in that quarter.

The registration requirements operate in the same manner as for ISO. In fact, most of the registrar companies who certify organizations to ISO also can certify them to TL 9000. As with ISO, TL 9000 has been embraced by most Telecom companies all over the world. Over 350 companies have been registered so far.

The basic TL 9000 model is given in Figure B1.

More details on TL 9000 can be obtained from www.Questforum.org.

QS 9000

Just like TL 9000 is specific to the Telecom industry, QS 9000 is specific to the Automotive industry. Put together by the big three Automotive companies—General Motors Corporation, Ford Motor

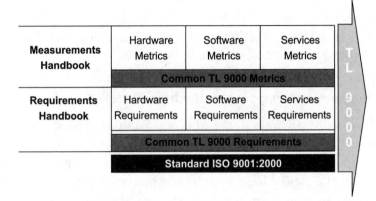

Fig. B1 TL 9000 Architecture

Company, and Chrysler Corporation (now Daimler Chrysler DCA)—QS 9000 was mandated by these companies for all their suppliers.

QS 9000 also rides on the basic ISO framework, with some specific and significant adders for the automotive industry. These are based on the Original Equipment Manufacturer (OEM) requirements for production parts and related services received from a large and multitier base of suppliers.

First released in 1994, QS 9000 comprises two sections—general requirements and customer-specific requirements. There are a number of associated reference manuals to support the QS 9000 manual. Six reference manuals—the Quality System Assessment (QSA), Advanced Quality Planning and Control Plan (APQP), Failure Modes and Effects Analysis (FMEA), Measurement System Analysis (MSA), Production Part Approval Process (PPAP), and Statistical Process Control (SPC)—are considered integral for applying the specific compliance requirements of the QSR.

Just like the Quest forum for TL 9000, there is the Supplier Quality Requirements task force (SQRTF) for QS 9000. This group operates on behalf of the Big Three and also works with the Automotive Supplier Association and Automotive Industry Action Group (AIAG). The SQRTF has designated Plexus Corporation of St. Paul, Minnesota, as the QS 9000 sanctioned training provider for auditor qualification training and examination.

QS 9000 is being replaced by ISO/TS 16949, last revised in 2002.

A good reference manual, covering in detail all of the above models, is the latest edition of the ISO Handbook, *The ISO 9000 Handbook*—Fourth Edition—Robert W. Peach.[2]

Comparison and Mapping to Baldrige Model

As discussed in Chapter 3, the Malcolm Baldrige criteria came into existence in 1987 and have since emerged as a holistic model with a focus on performance excellence relative to the business of any corporation. The Baldrige criteria have increased over the years and expanded such that we now have the criteria for health care and education, beyond the original criteria for business.

The focus of all the international models we discussed above is on quality processes and their management that result in a quality management system. However, the Baldrige criteria is a business management model. Therefore, the former is a subset of the latter. In the experience of the authors, a company certified to ISO 9000:2000, when assessed against the Baldrige model, would end up scoring roughly 350 to 400 points on the Baldrige scale of 1 to 1000 points. Figure B2 is an attempt to map the ISO/TL/QS 9000 elements to the Baldrige criteria. Note that not every element in the three quality system models has been mapped. This is because, in some cases, they are extremely low-level processes.

Legend

X indicates strong alignment

Y indicates weak alignment

Red indicates TL 9000 elements

Blue indicates QS 9000 elements

REFERENCES

(1) "The ISO 9000 Handbook," Fourth edition, Robert W. Peach, McGraw-Hill, Inc., USA, 2003.

(2) Ibid.

ISO 9000/ Baldrige Matrix	Leadership		Str. Plg.		Custo. & Mkt.		Info.& Anal.		HR Focus			Process Mgmt.		Business Results					
ISO 9000	1.1	1.2	2.1	2.2	3.1	3.2	4.1	4.2	5.1	5.2	5.3	6.1	6.2	7.1	7.2	7.3	7.4	7.5	7.6
4.QMS Req.	x		x	y	y				x	x	y	x	x	y	y	y	y	y	y
5.1 Mgmt. Commitment	x		x		x				x	x	x	x	x		y	y			y
5.1.1 Process** Effectivity	x											x							
5.2 Customer Focus	x		x		x	x							y						
5.2 Customer** Focus	x		x		x	x													
5.2.C.1 Customer-* Relationship Development	y				x	x													
5.2.C.2 Customer-* Communication Procedures	y				x	x							x						
5.3 Quality Policy			x									y	y						
5.4 Planning	x		y	x															
5.4.1.C.1 Quality* Objectives	x		x						y	y	y	y	y	y	y	y	y	y	y
5.4.2.C.1 Long-* and Short-term Planning	x		x	x															
5.4.2.C.2* Customer Input	x		x	x	x								y						
5.4.2.C.3 Supplier* Input	x		x	x									x					x	
5.5 Resp. Authority and Communication	x			y															
5.5.1.1 Stopping** Production for Quality Concerns	x											x							
5.6 Mgmt. Review	x		x	x								x	x	x	x		y	x	x
6.1 Provision of Resources	x		x						x	x	x						y		
6.2 Human Resources	x		x						x	x	x								
6.2.2.1 Product** Design Skills									y	x									
6.2.2.C.3 Training* Requirements and Awareness										x									
6.3 Infrastructure											x								
6.3.2 Contingency** Plans												y	y						
6.4 Work Environment											x								
7.1 Planning of Product Realization												x	x					y	y
7.1.C.1 Life Cycle* Model												x	x						
7.1.C.2 New* Product Introduction												x	x						
7.1.C.3 Disaster Recovery												x							

(Contd...)

Fig. B2 Map of ISO/TL/QS 9000 Elements to the Baldrige Criteria

Legend
X indicates strong alignment
Y indicates weak alignment
* indicates TL 9000 elements
** indicates QS 9000 elements

(Contd.)

ISO 9000/ Baldrige Matrix	Leadership		Str. Plg.		Custo. & Mkt.		Info.& Anal.		HR Focus			Process Mgmt.		Business Results					
ISO 9000	1.1	1.2	2.1	2.2	3.1	3.2	4.1	4.2	5.1	5.2	5.3	6.1	6.2	7.1	7.2	7.3	7.4	7.5	7.6
7.2 Customer Related Processes					y	y						x							
7.2.2.2** Manufacturing Feasibility		y		y								y							
7.3 Design and Development												x	x		x				x
7.3.6.3 Product** Approval Process												y							
7.4 Purchasing													x					x	
7.4.1.C.1 Purchasing* Procedures													x					x	
7.4.1.2 Supplier** QMS												y							
7.5 Production and Service Provision												x	x						
7.5.1.5** Management of Production Tooling												y	y						
7.6 Control of Measuring Devices													x						
8.1 Measurement, Analysis and Improvement						x													
8.2.1 Customer Satisfaction						x								y					
8.2.1.C.1* Customer-Satisfaction Data						x	x							x					
8.2.2 Internal Audit												y	y						
8.2.3 Monitoring and Measurement of Processes					x	x			x	x	x	x	x						y
8.2.4 Monitoring and Measurement of Product												x	x						y
8.3 Control of Nonconforming Product												x	x						
8.4 Analysis of Data						x													
8.4.C.1 Trend Analysis* of Nonconforming Product						x						x	x		x				
8.4.H.1 Field* Performance Data						x						x	x		x				
8.5.1 Continuous Impt	x		x		x	x	x		y	y	y	x	x	y	y		y	y	y
8.5.1.C.1 Quality* Improvement Program	x		x			x			y	y	y	x	x	y	y		y	y	y
8.5.2/3 Corrective and Preventive Action						x						x	x					x	

INDEX

AUTHORS' PROFILES

Steven H. (Steve) Hoisington has been the Vice President of Quality for the Controls Business of Johnson Controls, Inc., in Milwaukee, Wisconsin, since 1999. He is responsible for developing and deploying a worldwide quality strategy that includes elements for ISO 9000, customer satisfaction surveys, quality measurement and reporting, and Six Sigma. Prior to joining Johnson Controls, Steve managed quality and customer satisfaction at IBM. He served as an examiner for the Malcolm Baldrige National Quality Award from 1992 to 2004, is a certified Six Sigma Black Belt, and recently co-authored a book entitled *Customer Centered Six Sigma*. He has authored numerous articles published in international trade magazines and is a frequent speaker at international conferences.

Steve received a Bachelor's degree in Industrial Engineering Technology from the University of Wisconsin and a Master's degree in Business Administration (MBA) from Winona State University. He is member of the Institute of Industrial Engineers, American Society for Quality, and serves as the chair on the board of directors for the Wisconsin Forward (Quality) Award.

S. A. Vaneswaran (SA) is currently with Lucent Technologies, USA. His current responsibilities include Registration and Maintenance of TL 9000 and ISO 14000 Quality and Environmental Systems, and driving Business Excellence Processes. He is also on the panel of examiners as part of the Quality New Jersey (QNJ) Governor's Award for Performance Excellence for the last five years.

SA has over three decades of experience in the areas of Total Quality. Before moving to USA in 1999, he was CEO of Tata Quality Management Services (TQMS), a division of Tata Sons in the Tata Group, where he set up the Tata Business Excellence Model (TBEM) process in the Group— this process is similar to the Malcolm Baldrige National Quality Award Process, and companies within the group participate in the Award Program. His responsibilities included coaching and training the group companies in the implementation of the MBNQA criteria. The TBEM Process is in its tenth year and is already a global benchmark.

SA has a Master's degree from IIT Madras, India. He was a key member of India's Space Program in the early eighties. He has served as a consultant to many companies in implementing the principles of Total Quality.